Mandala
Fantastic Coloring Book

Copyright: Published in the United States by Eric Tincher
Published January 2017
ISBN-13: 978 1542614795
ISBN-10: 1542614791

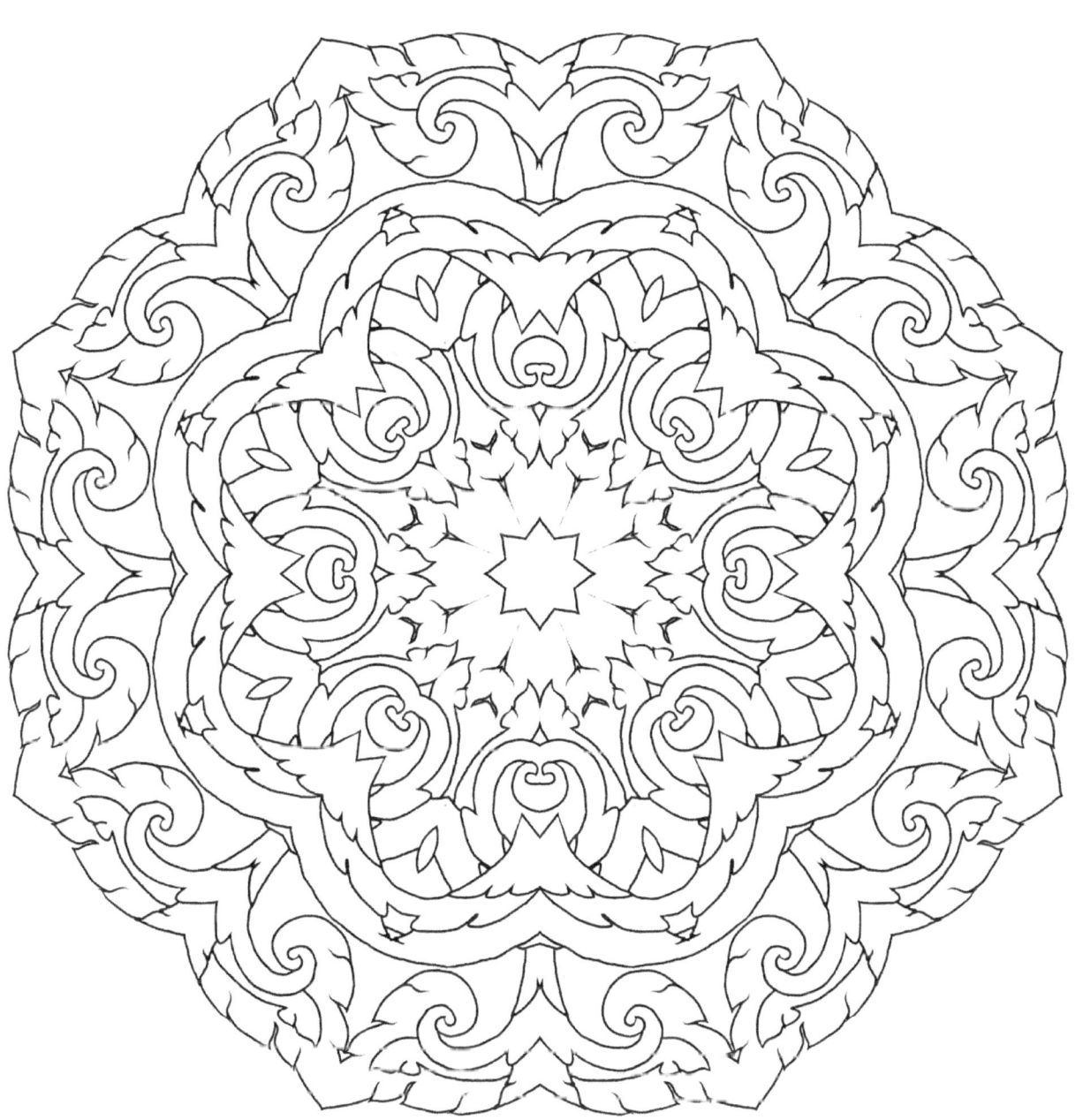

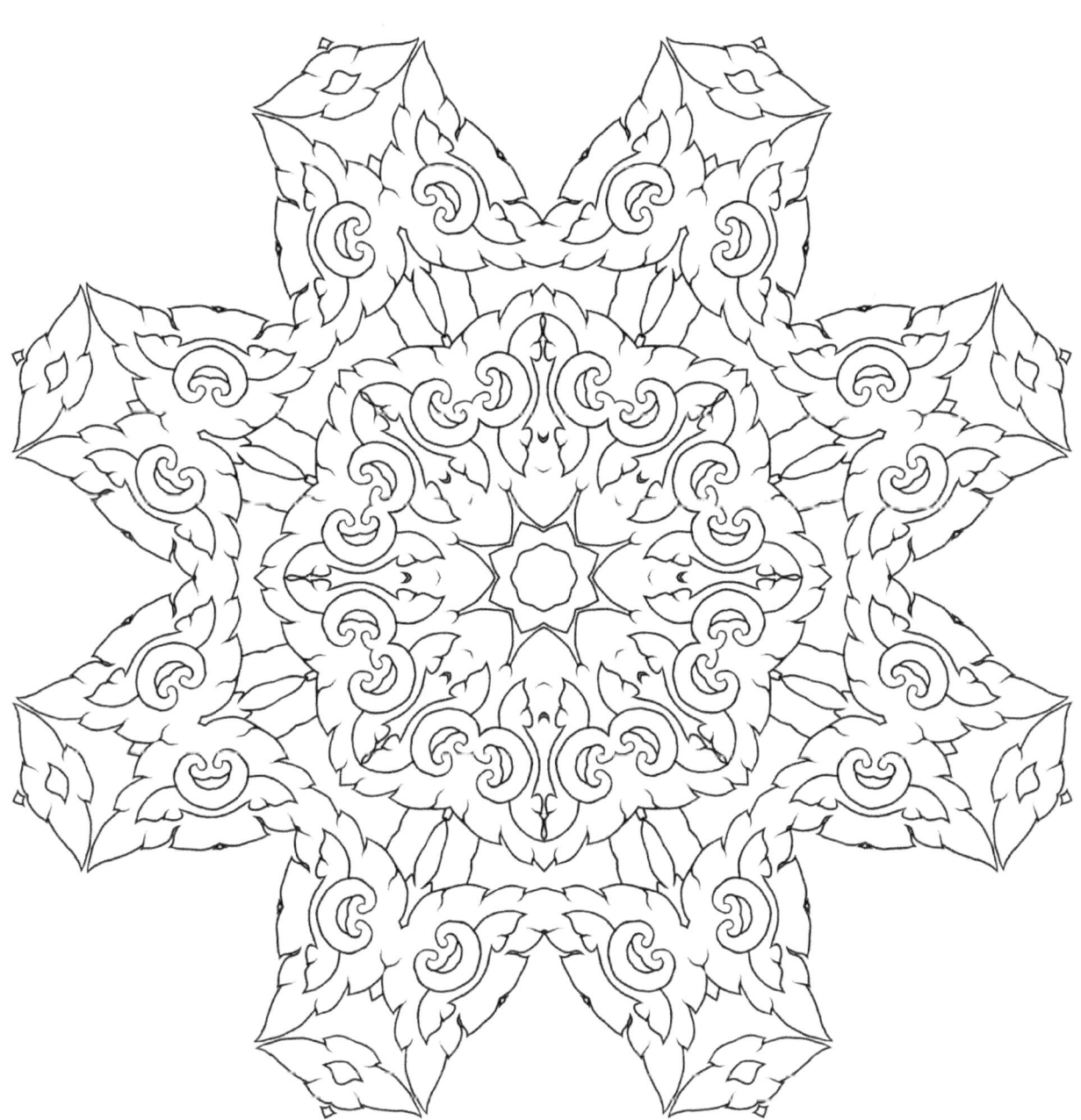

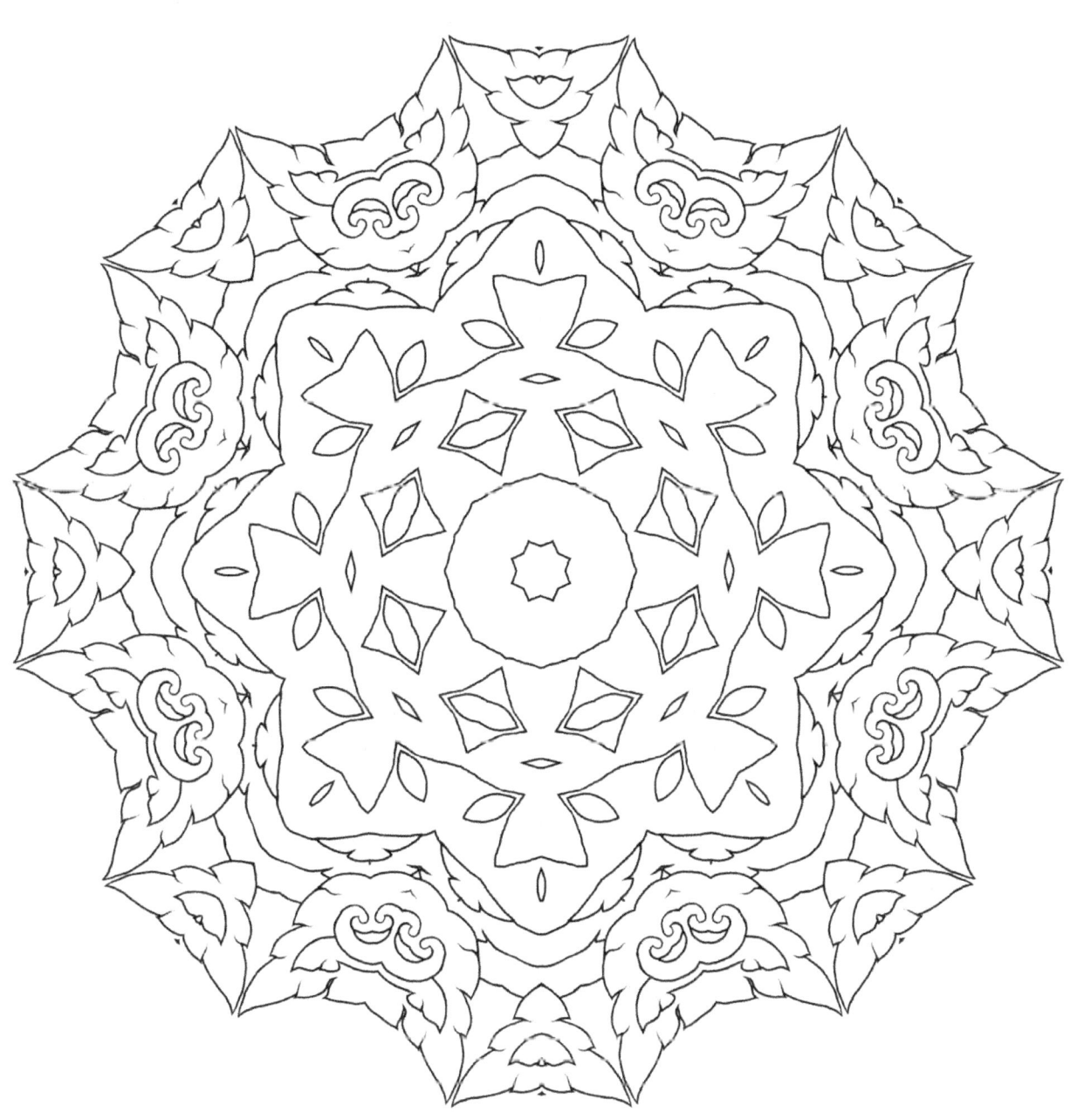

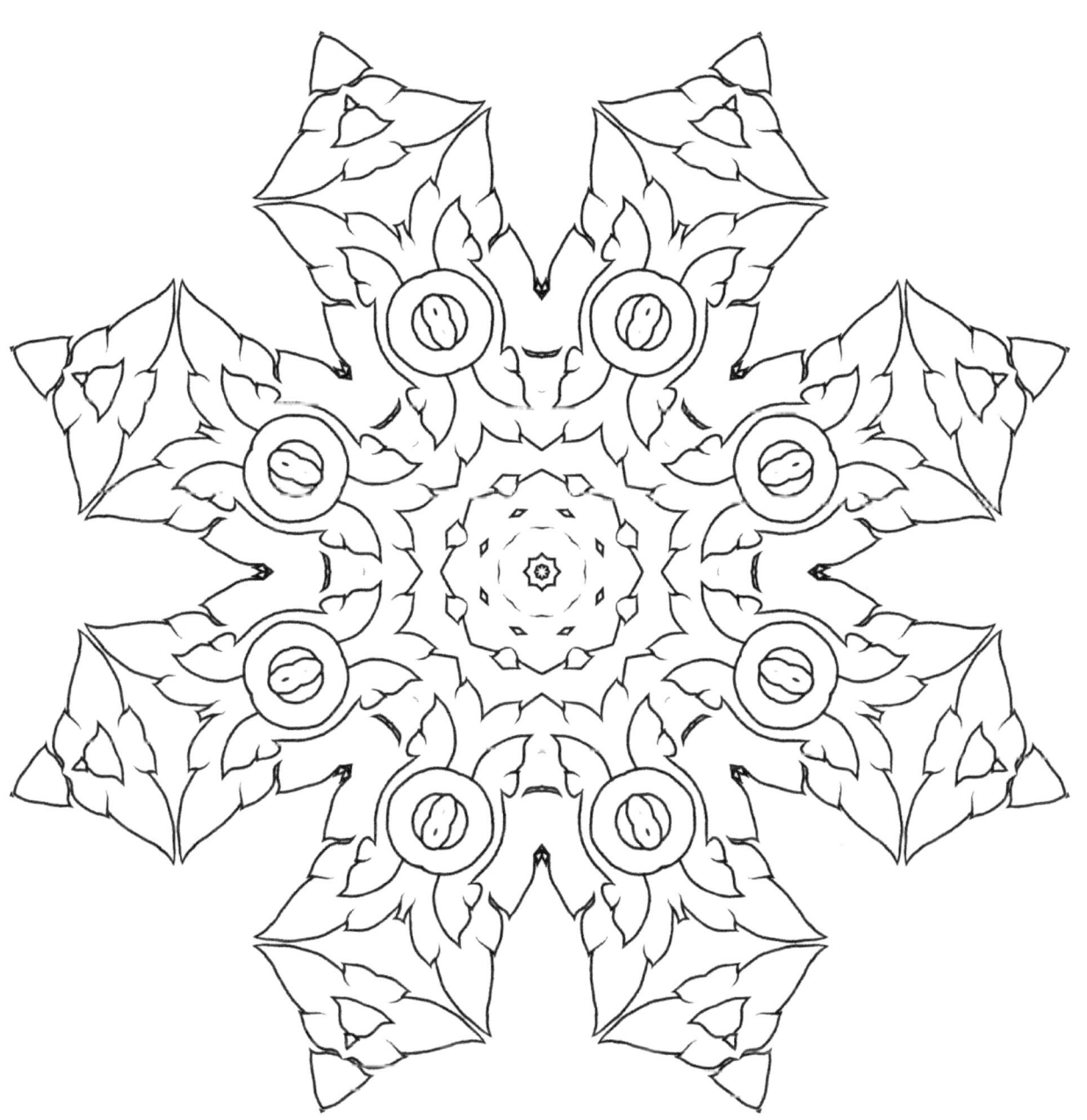

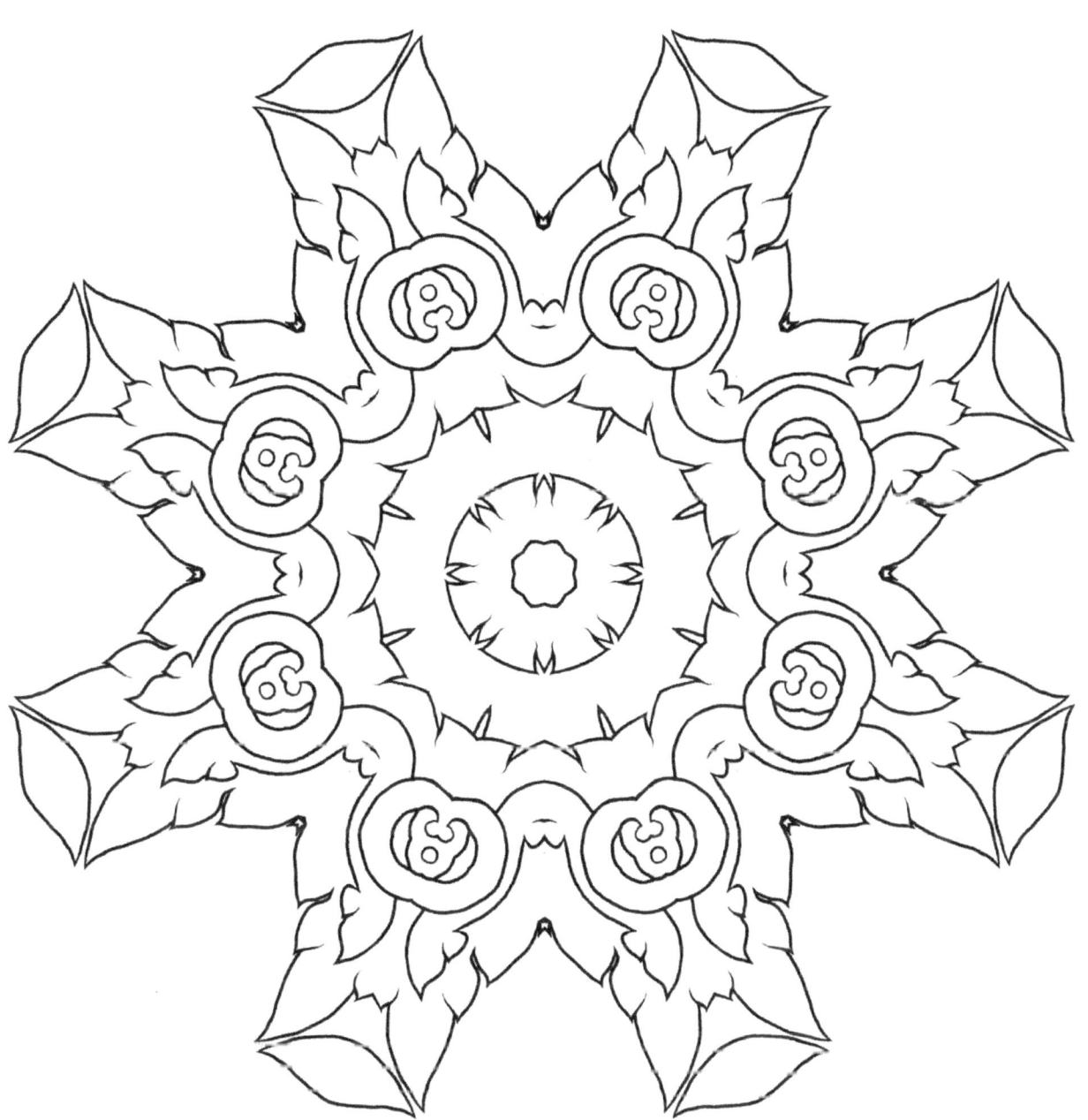

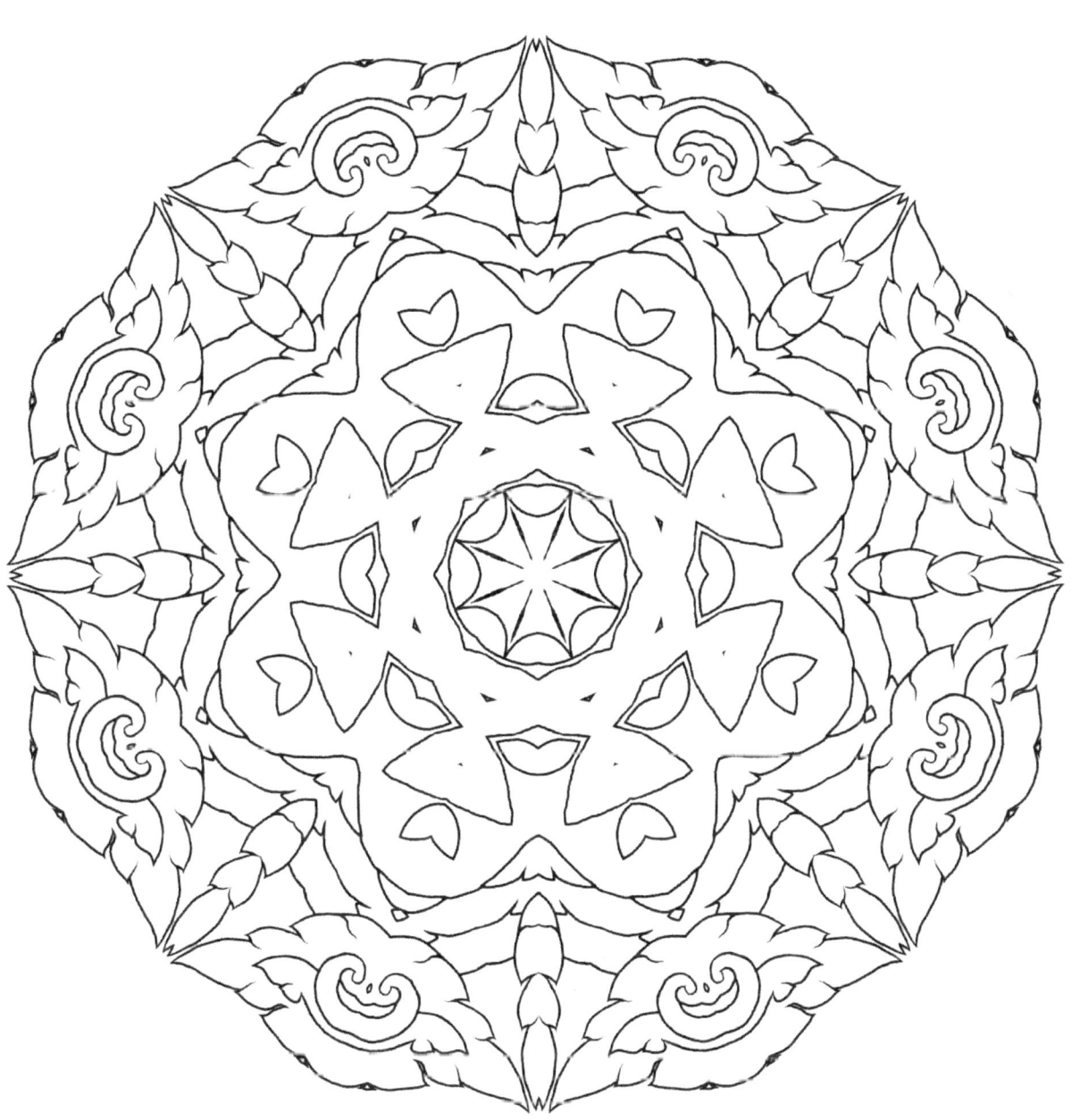

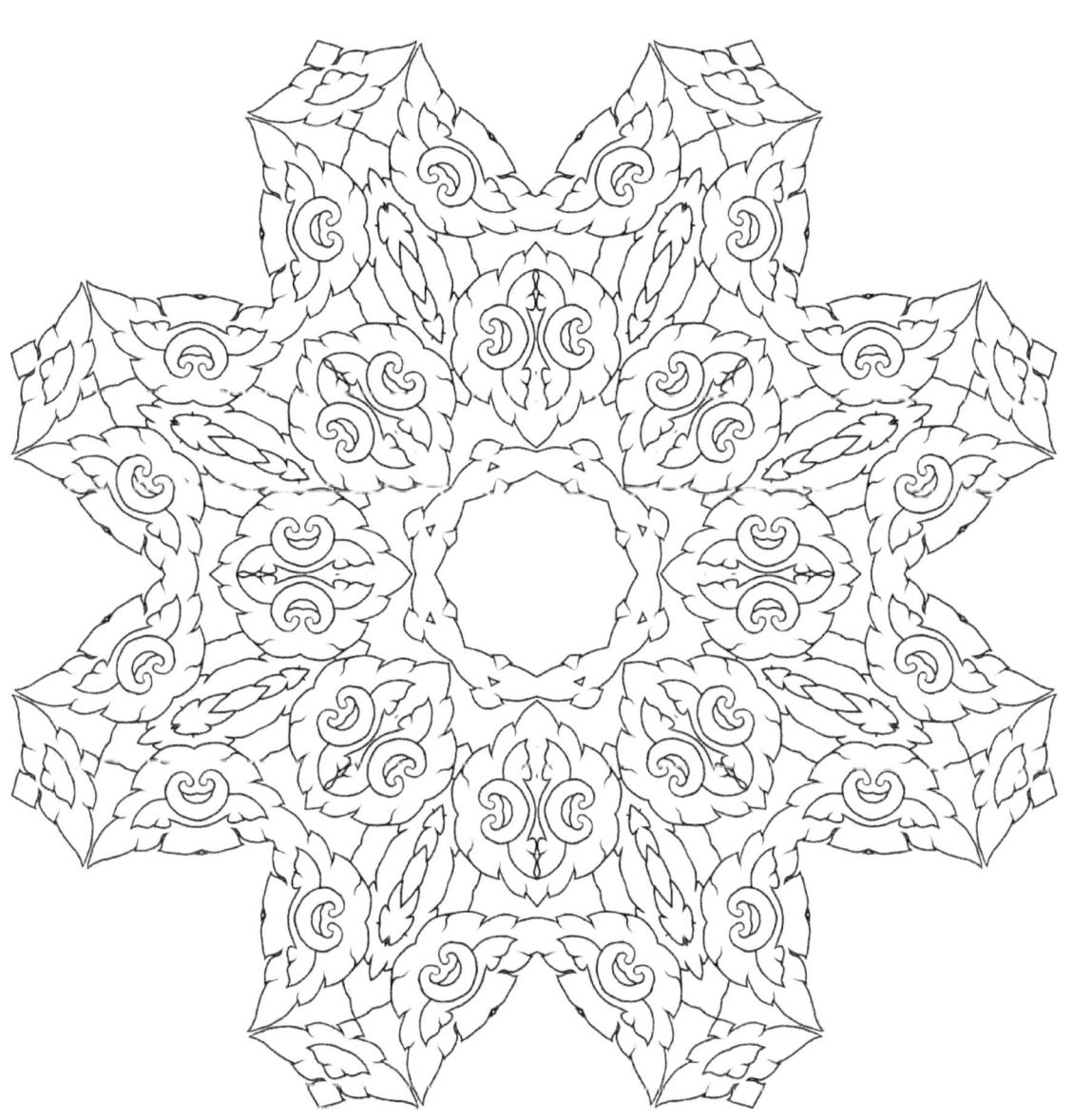

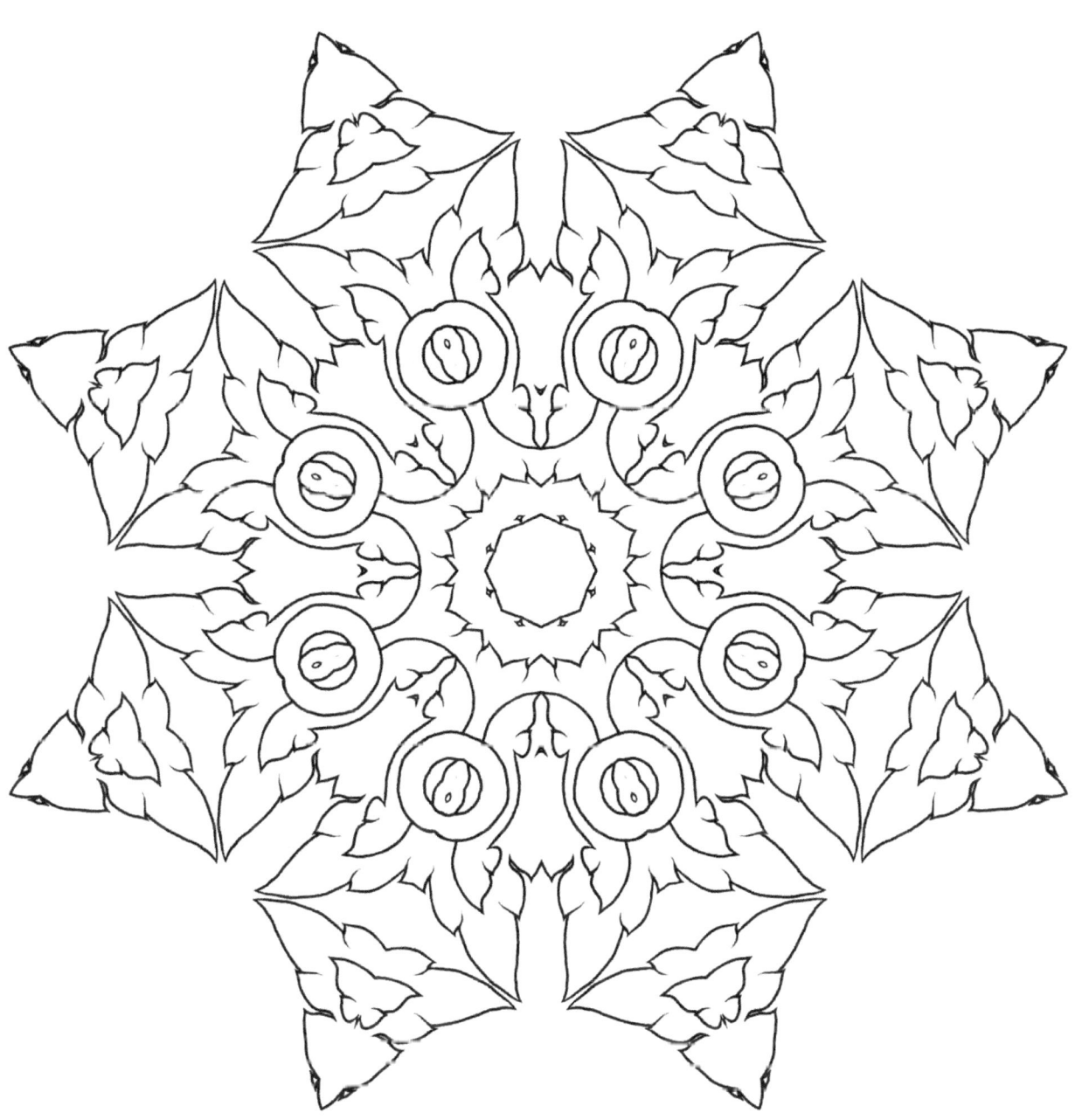

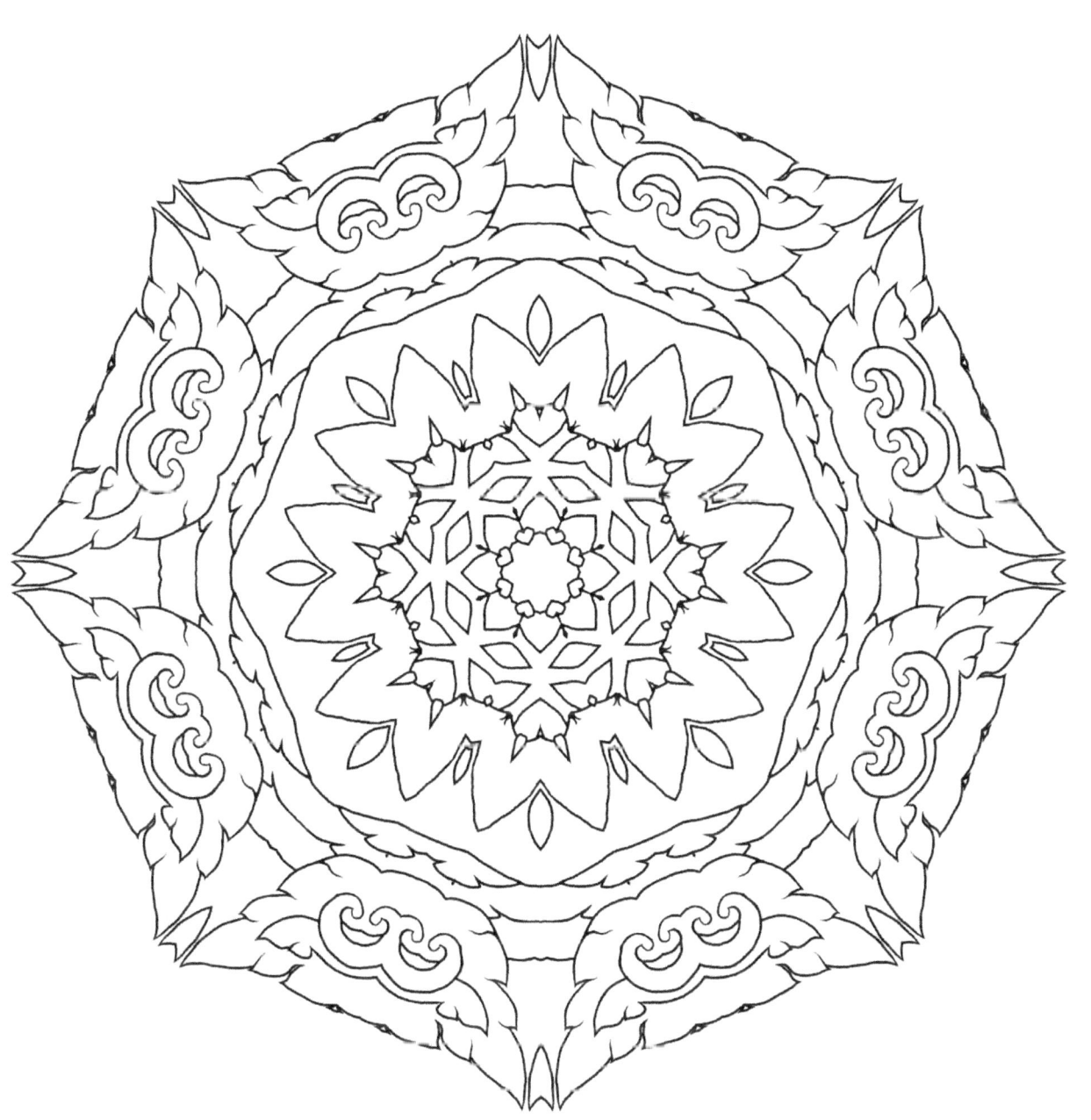

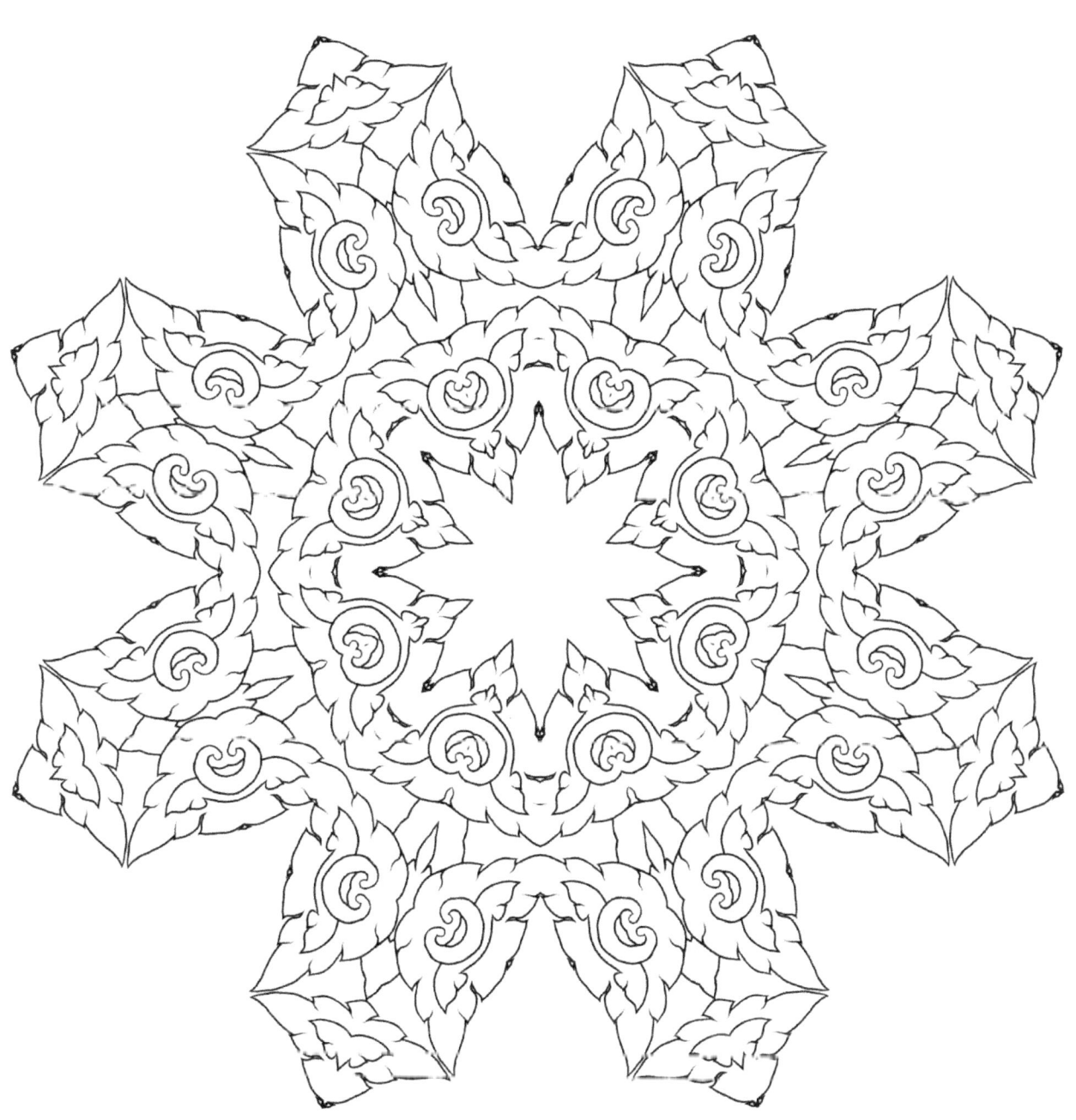

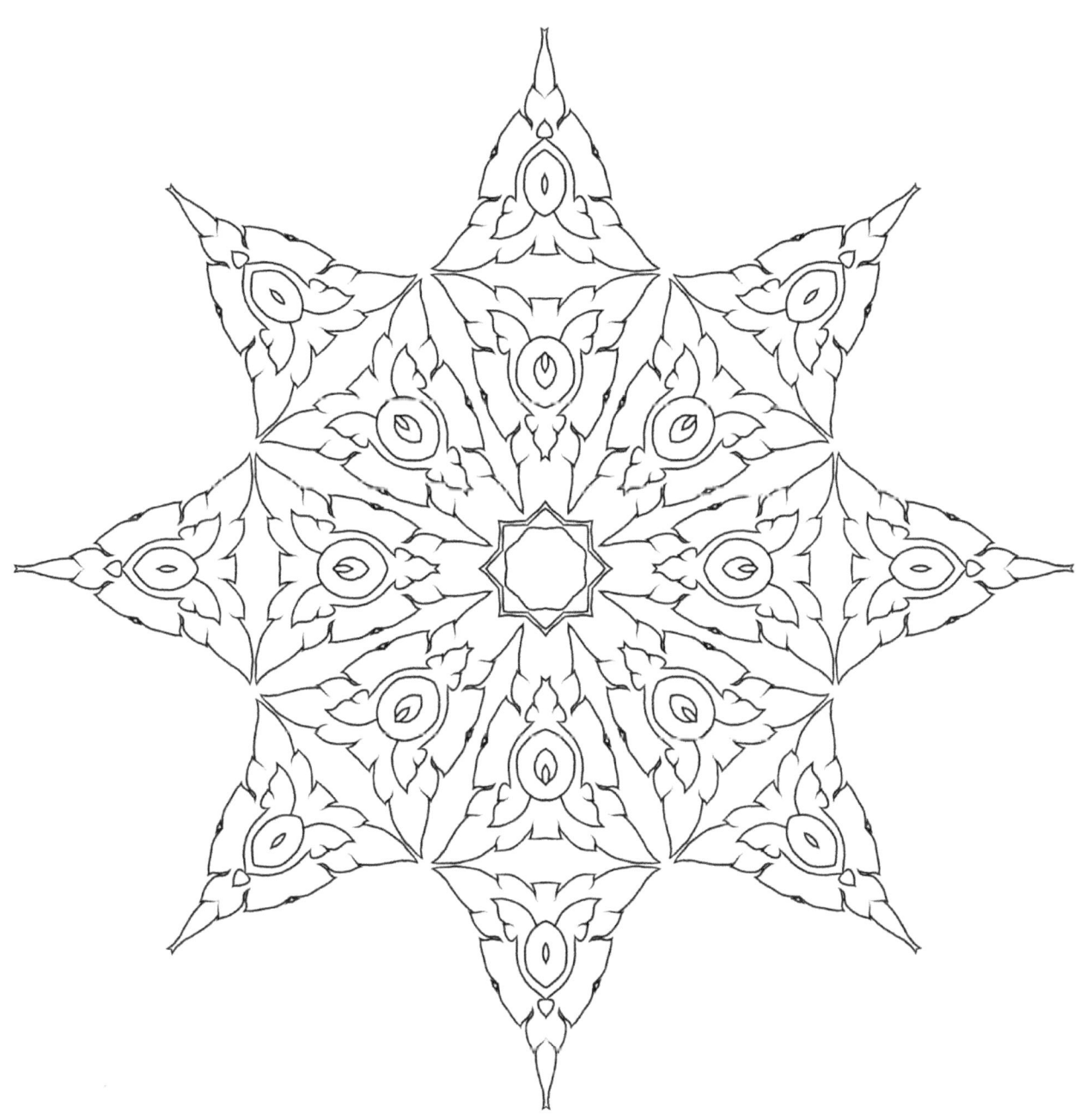

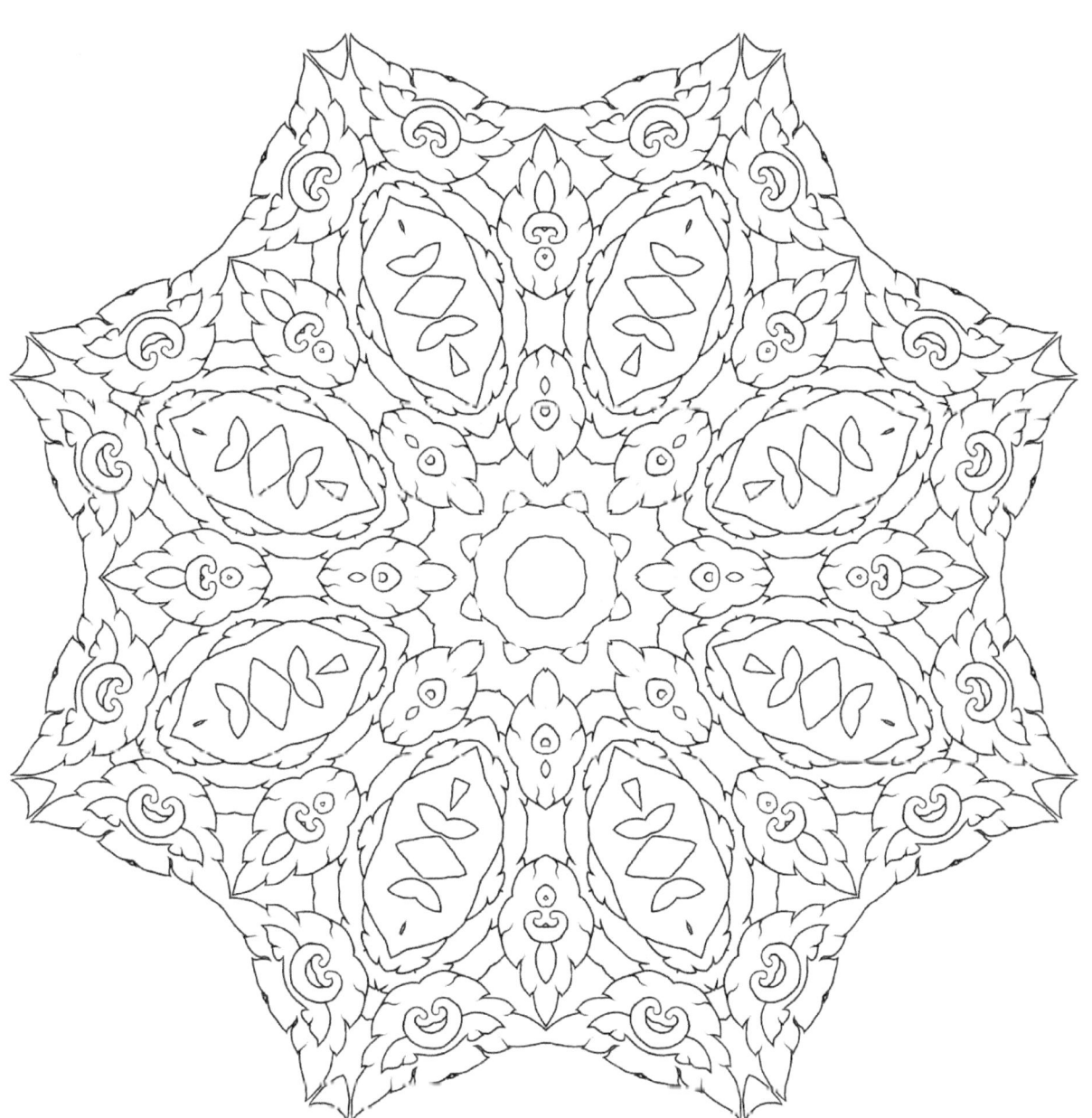

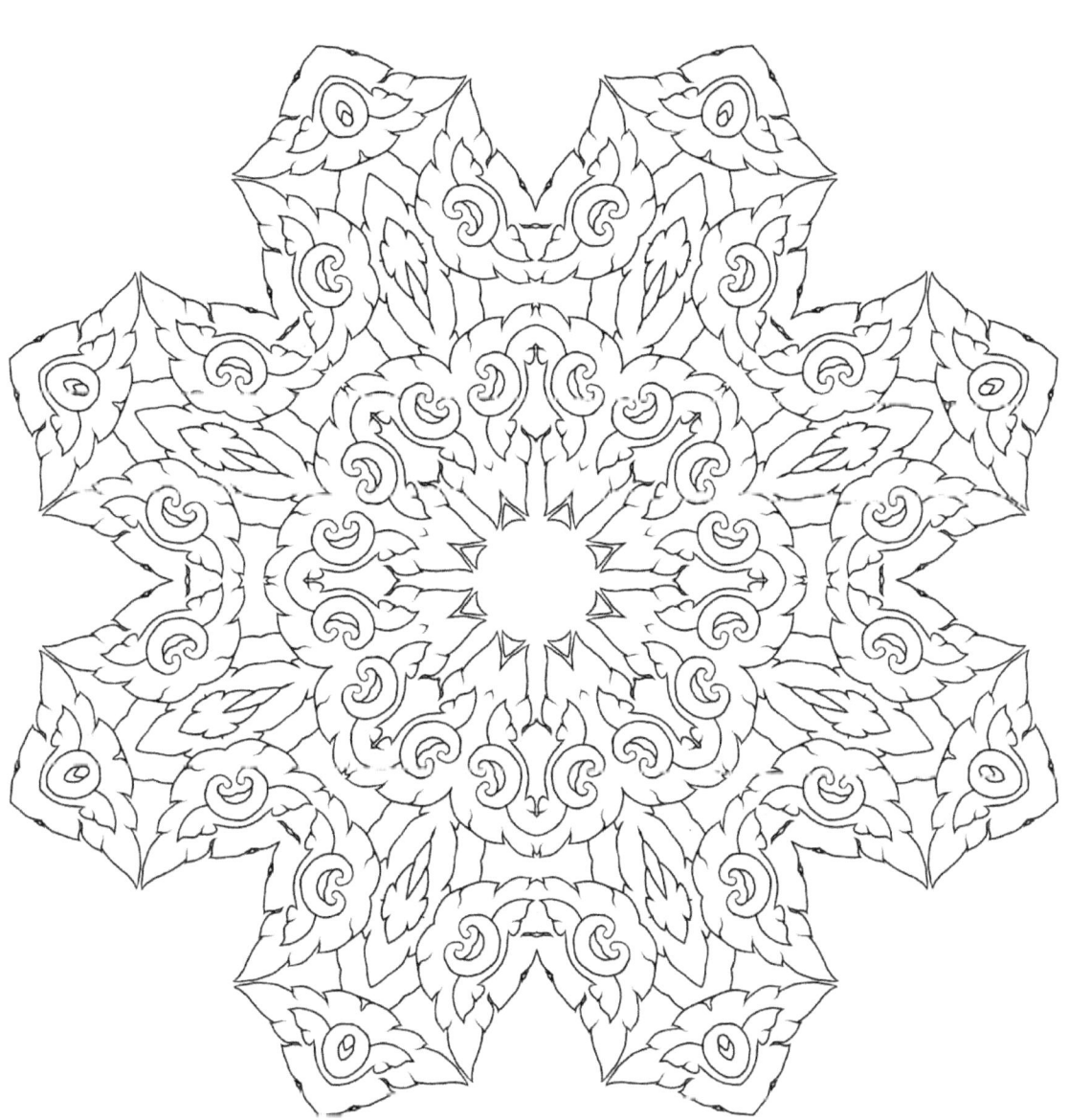

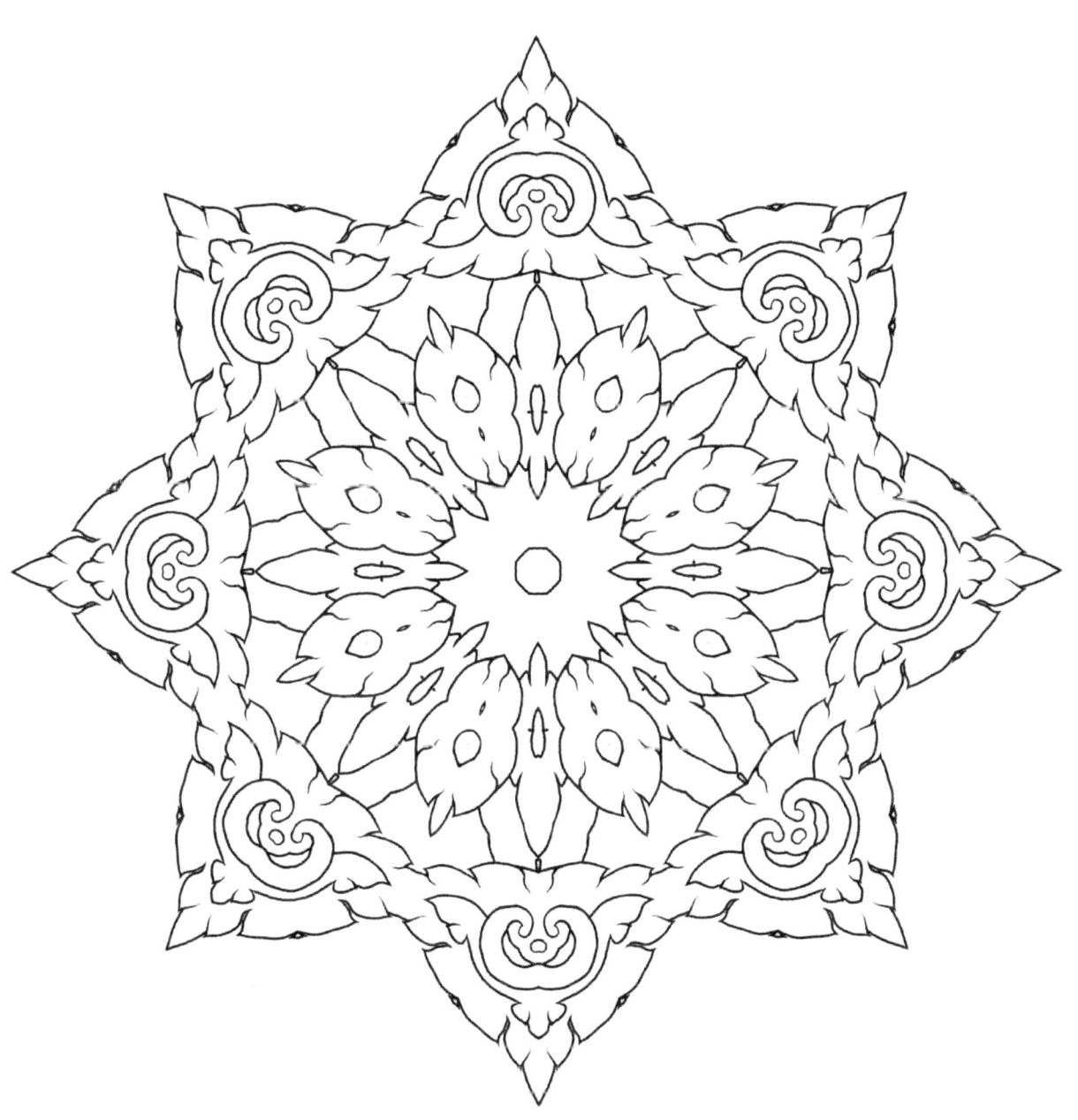

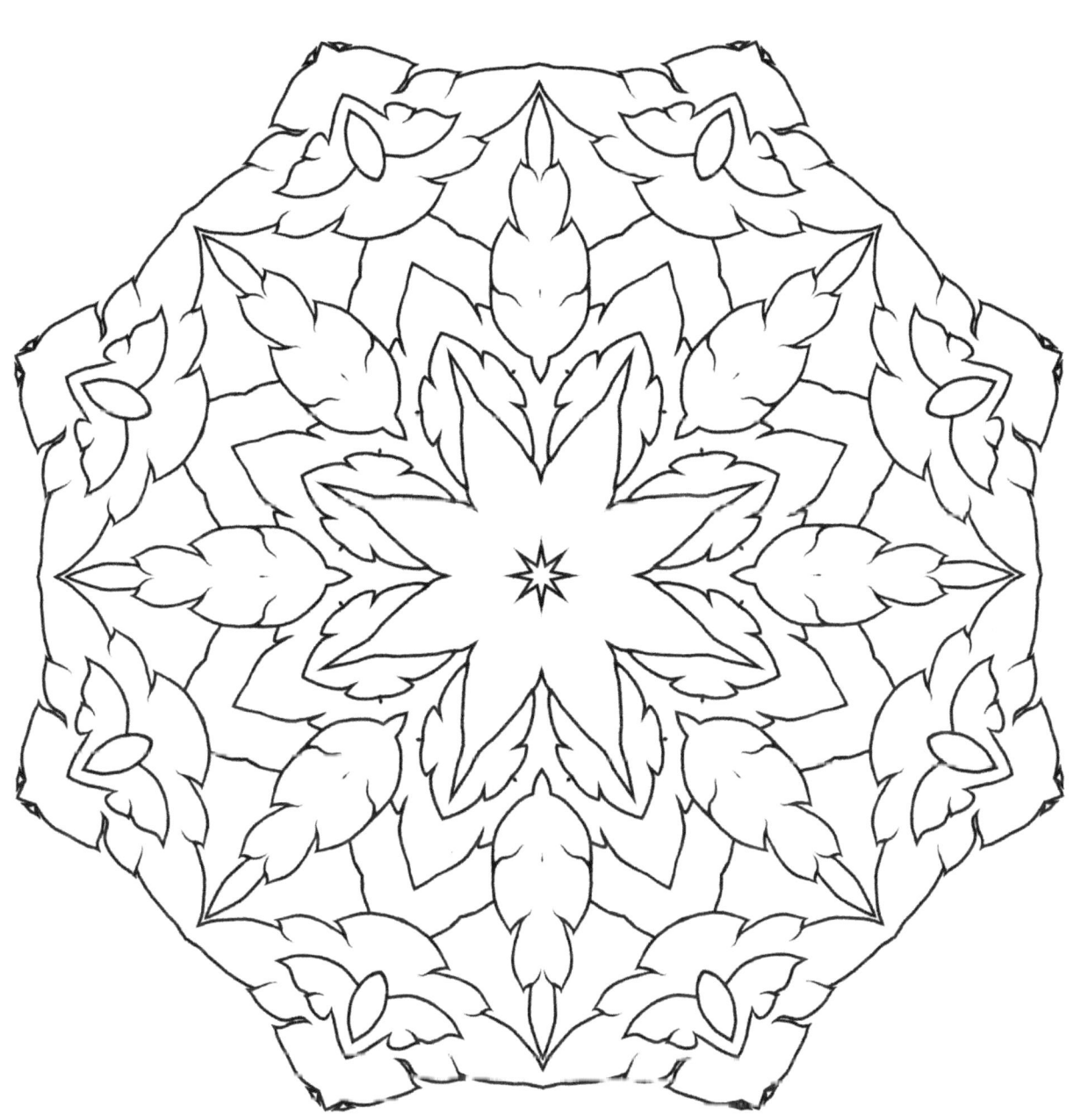

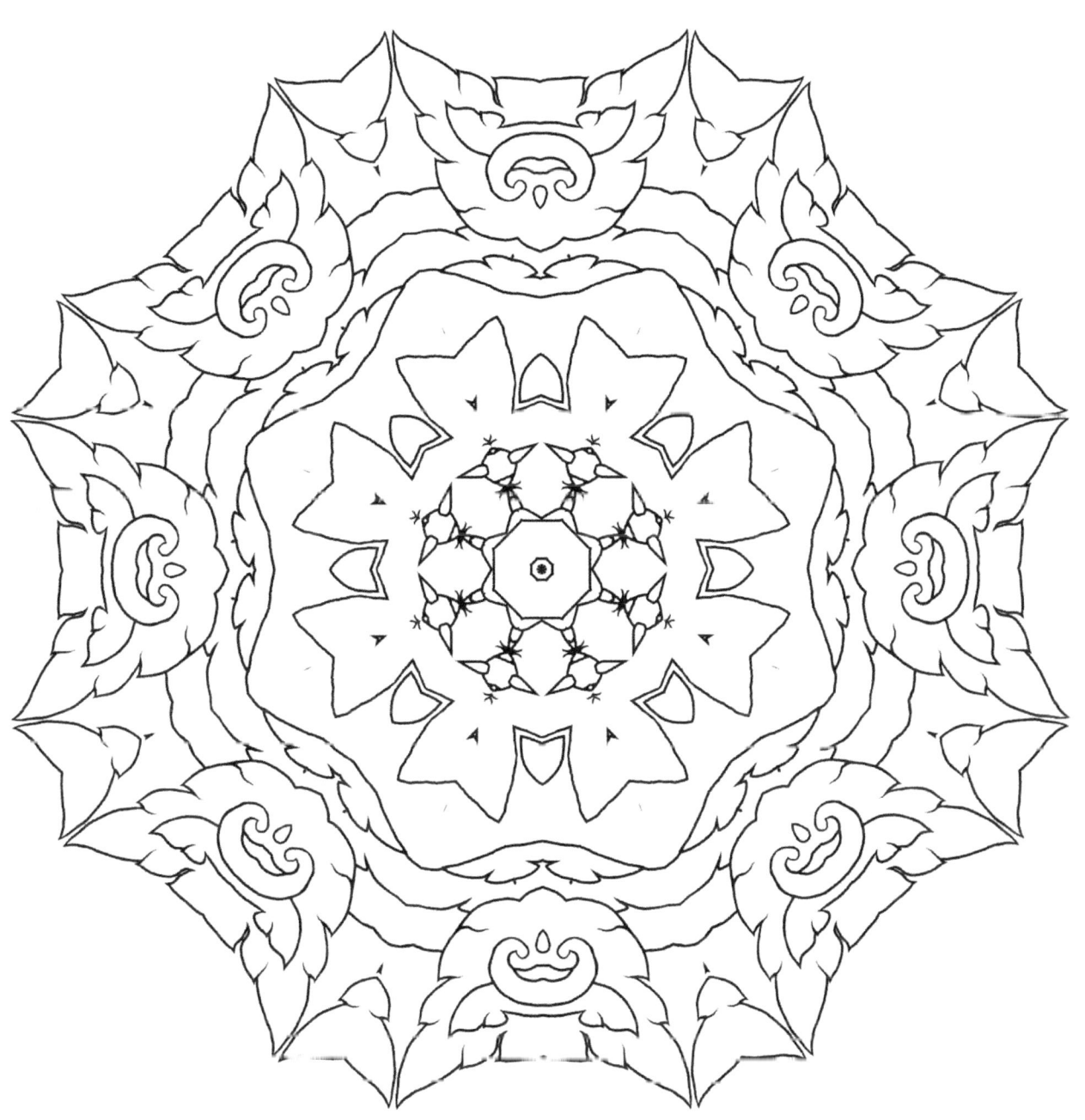

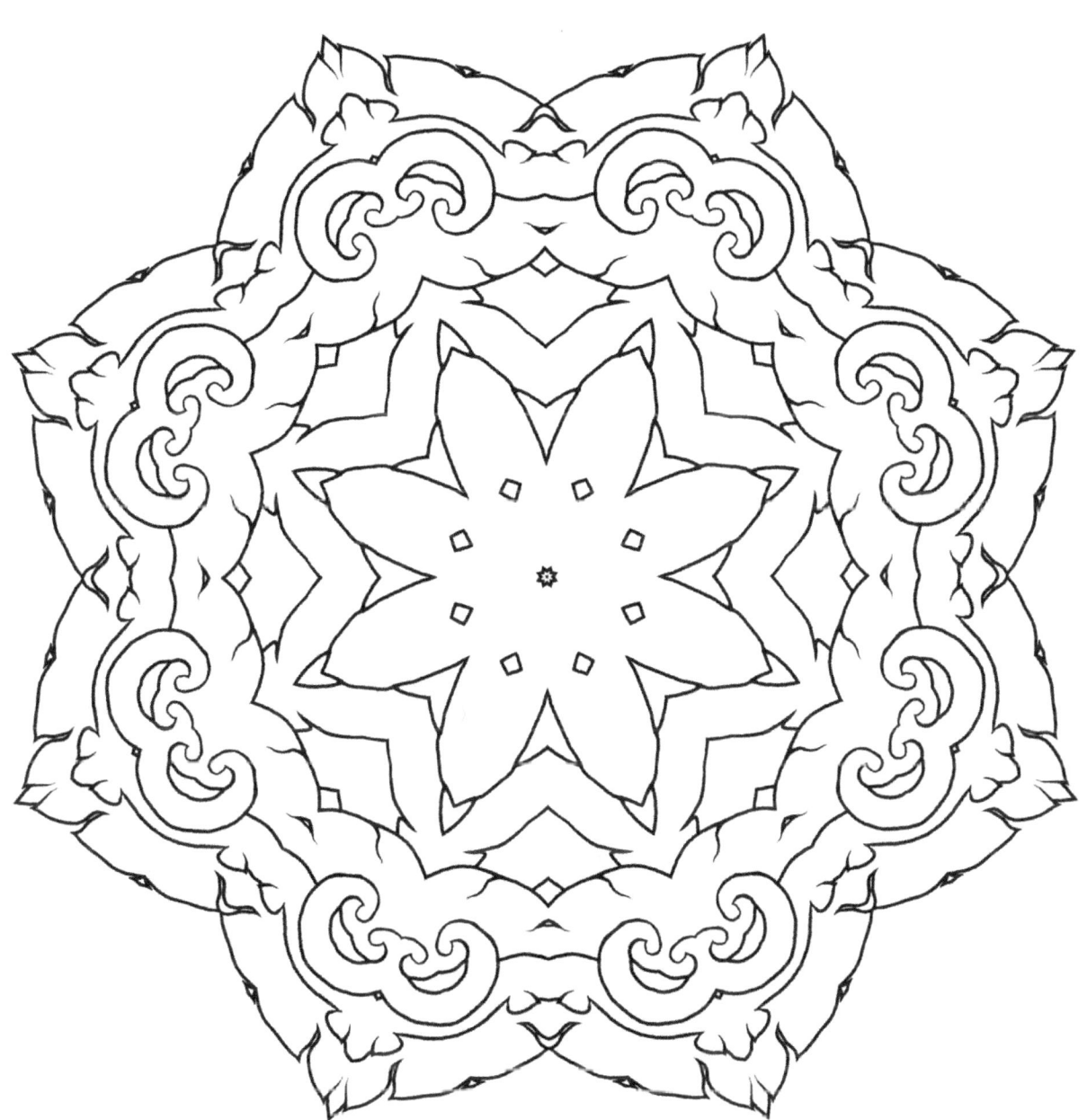

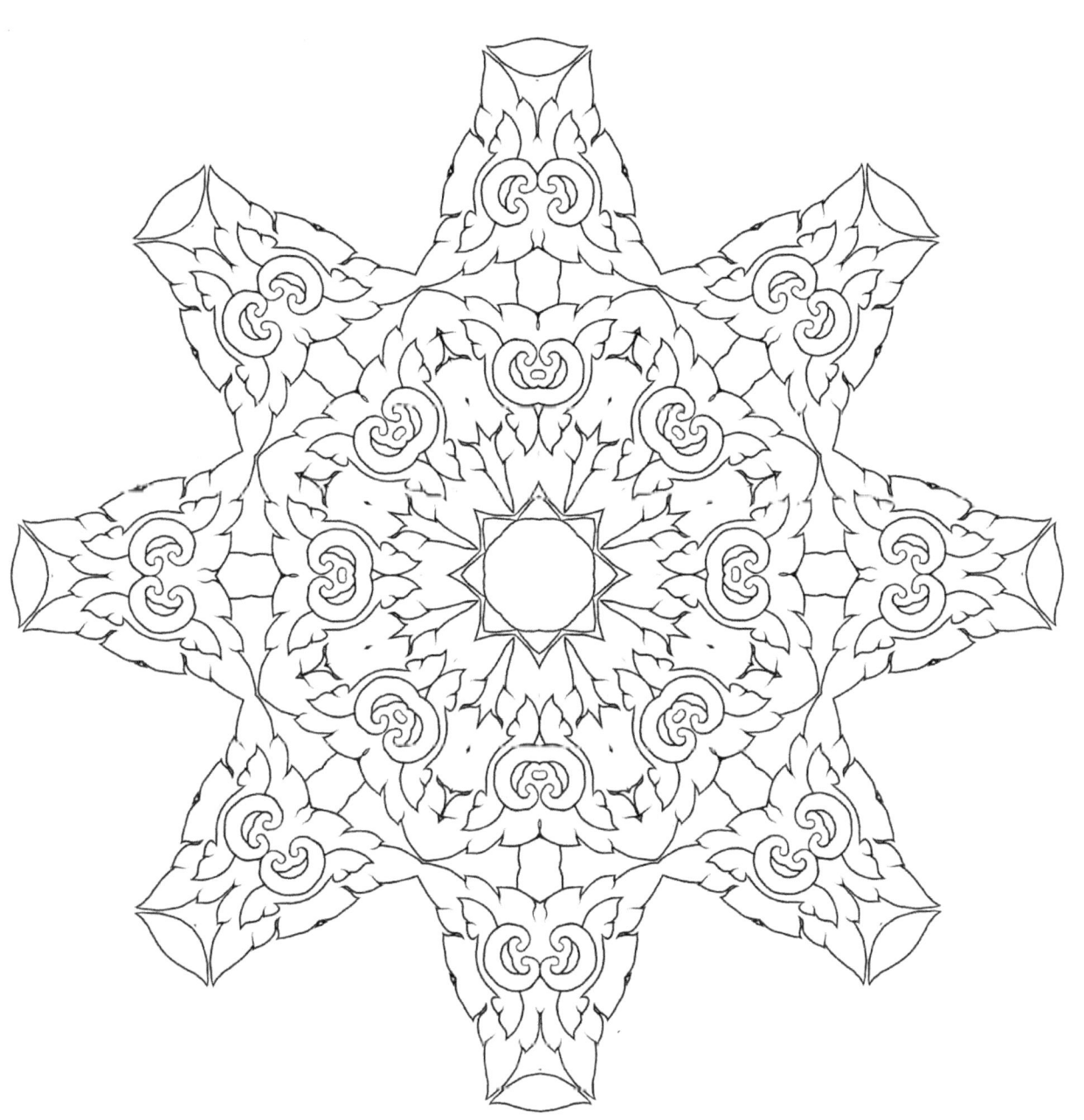

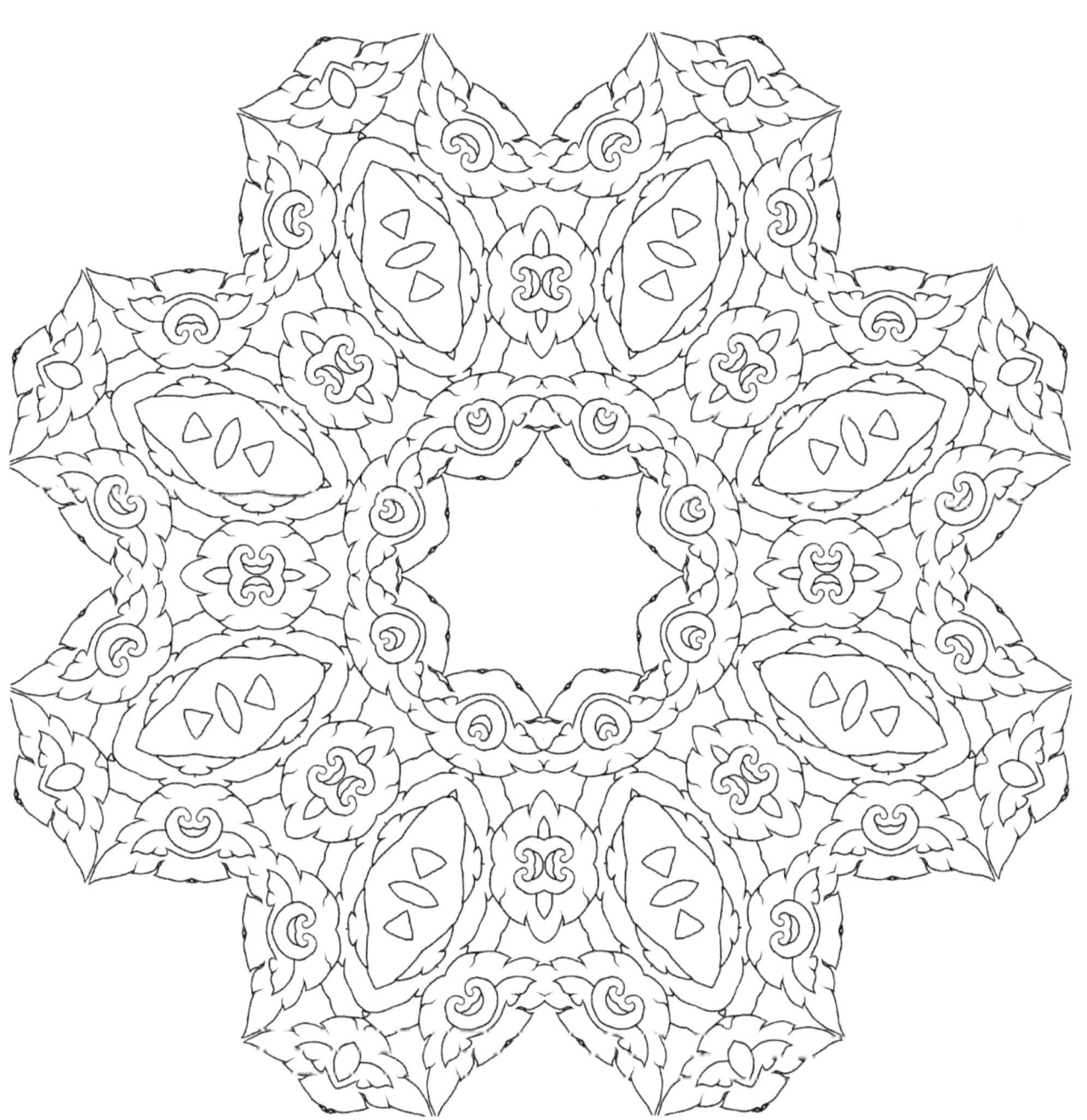

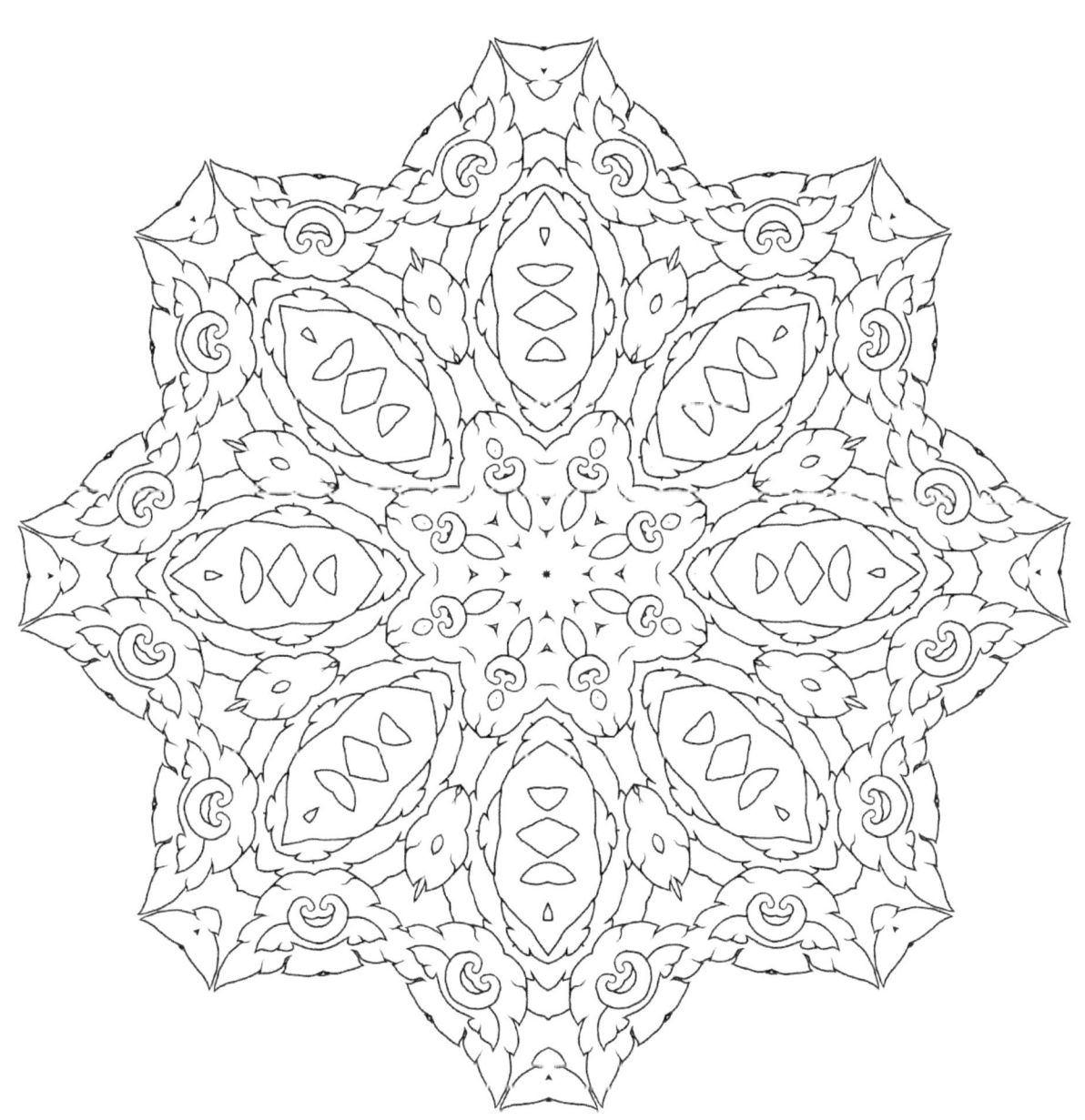

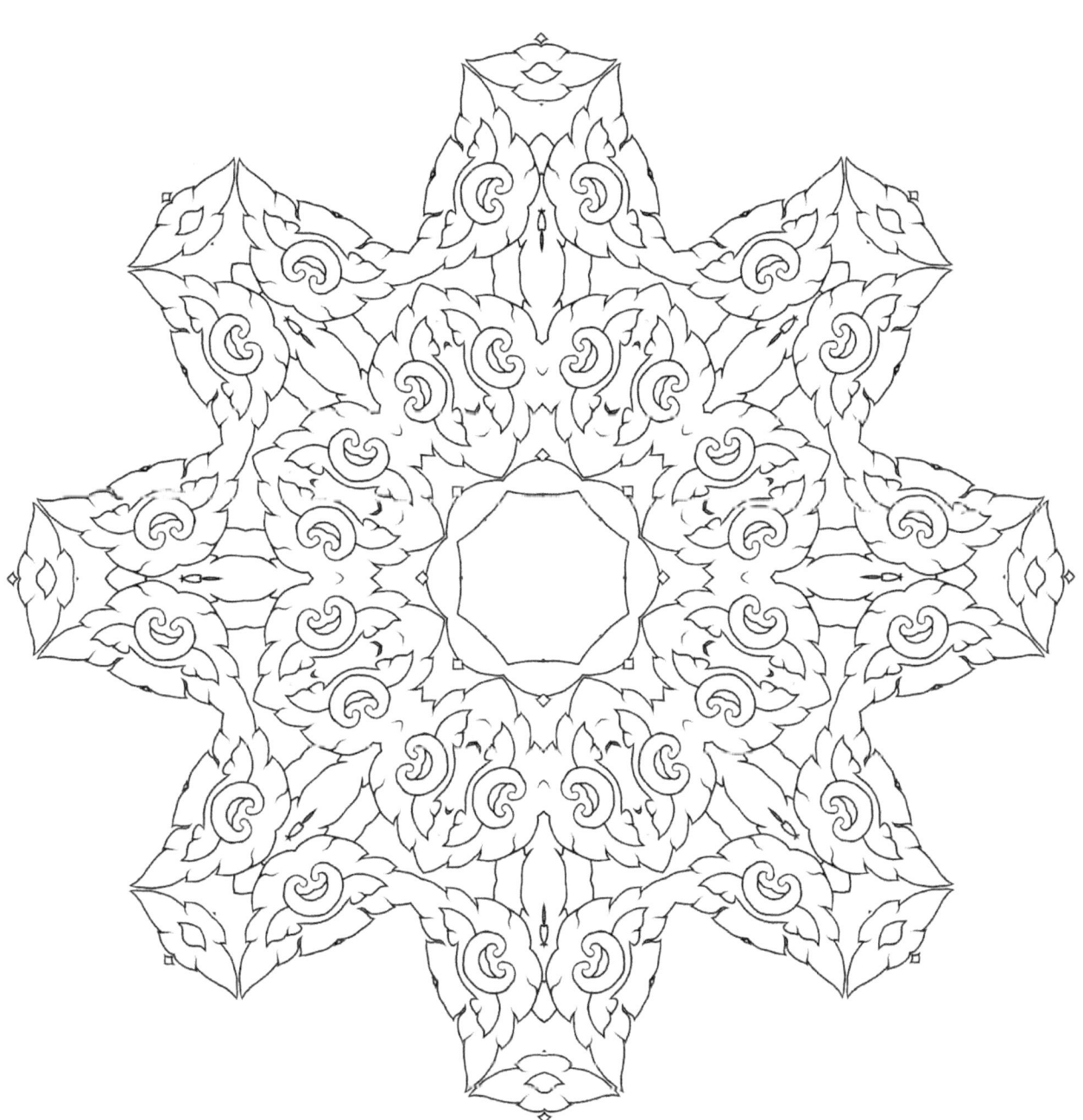

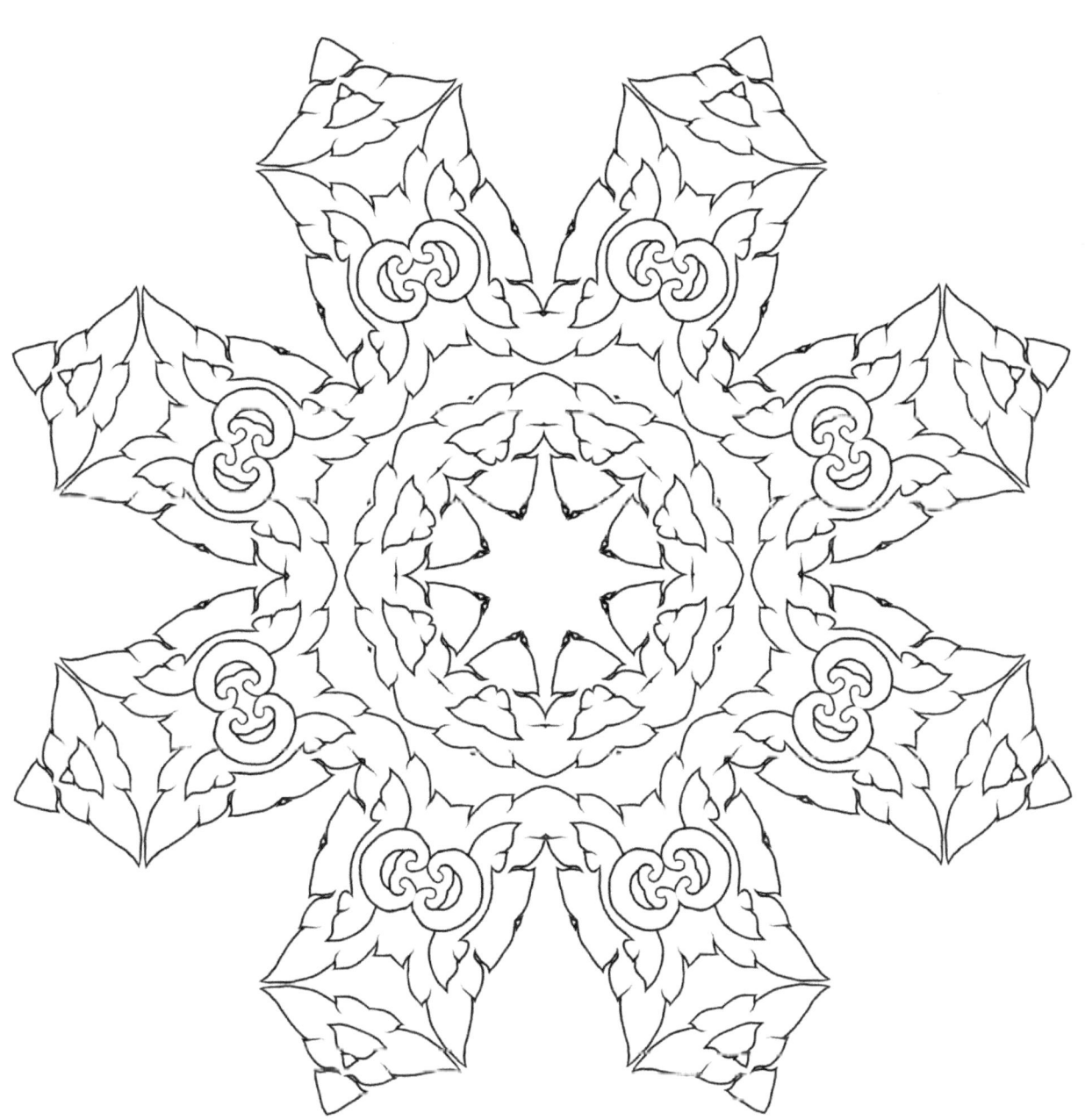

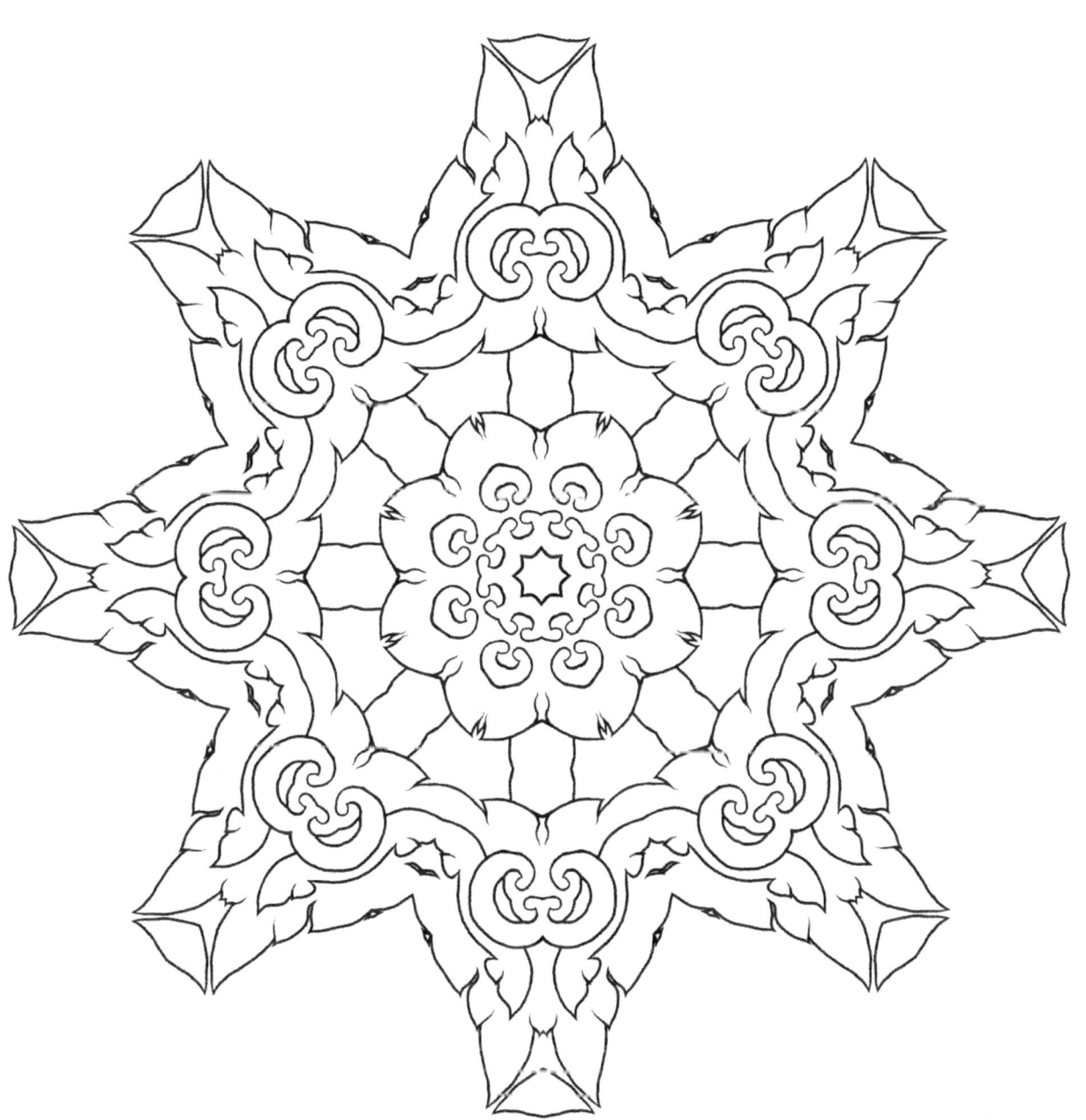

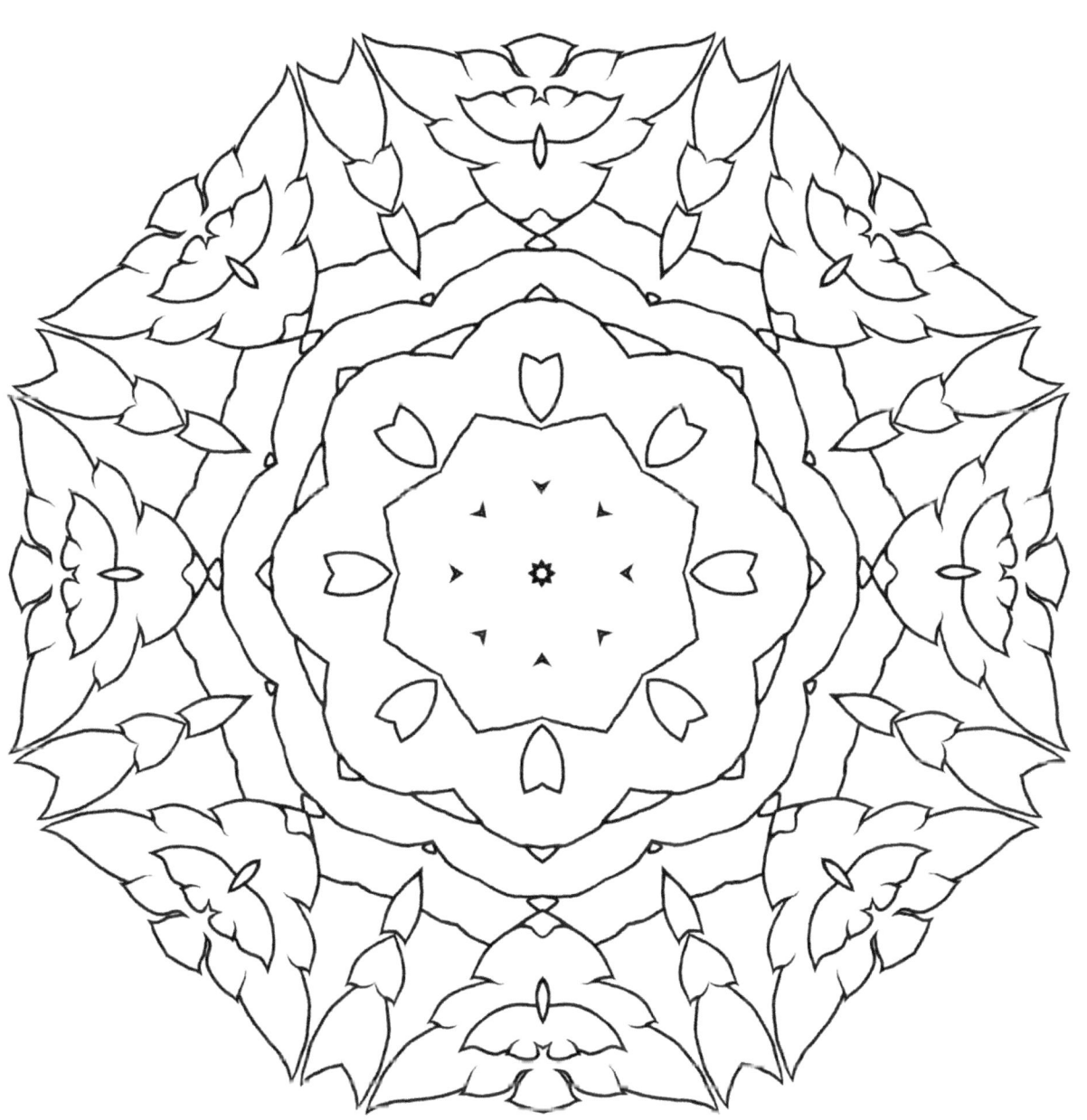

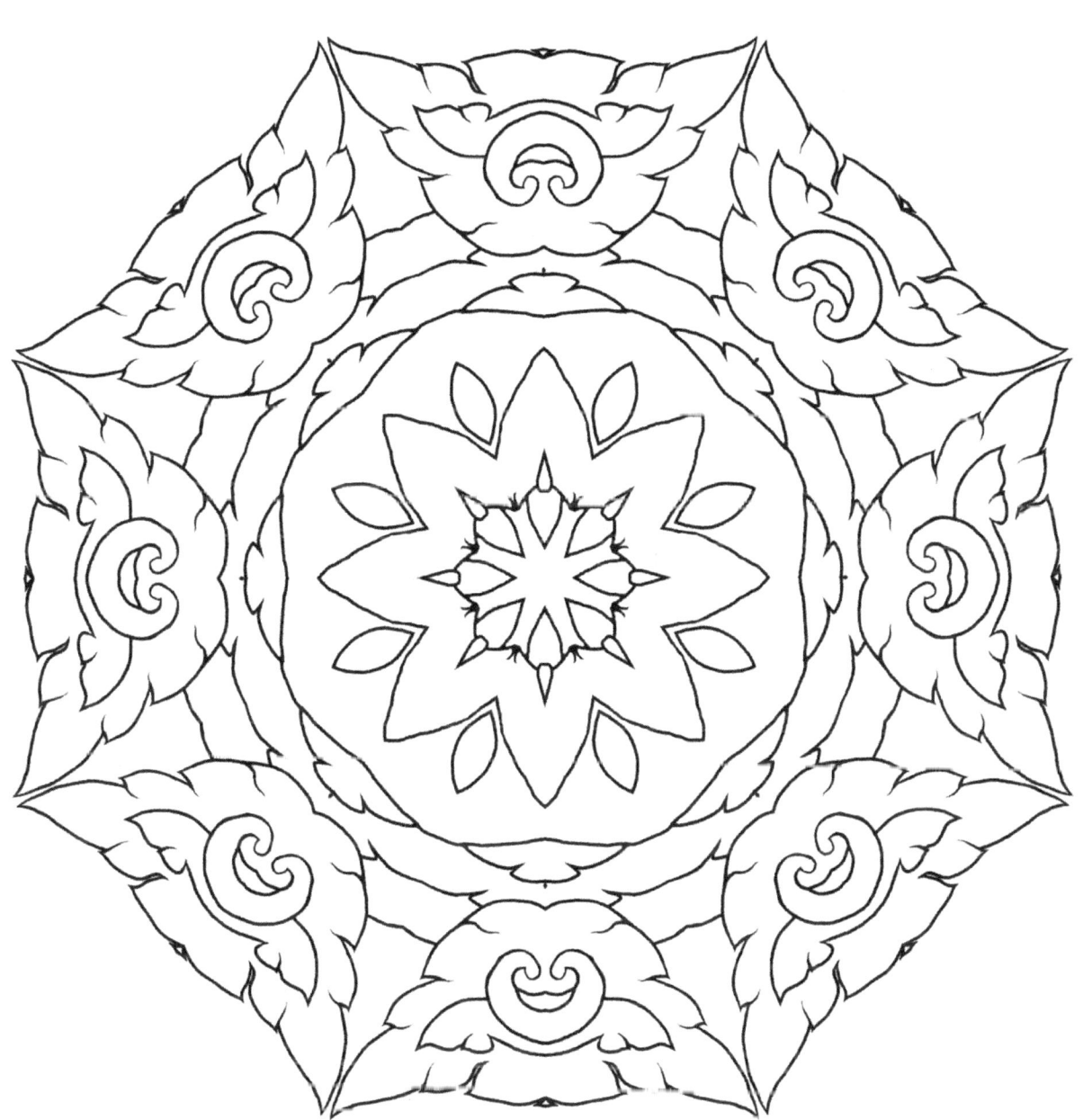

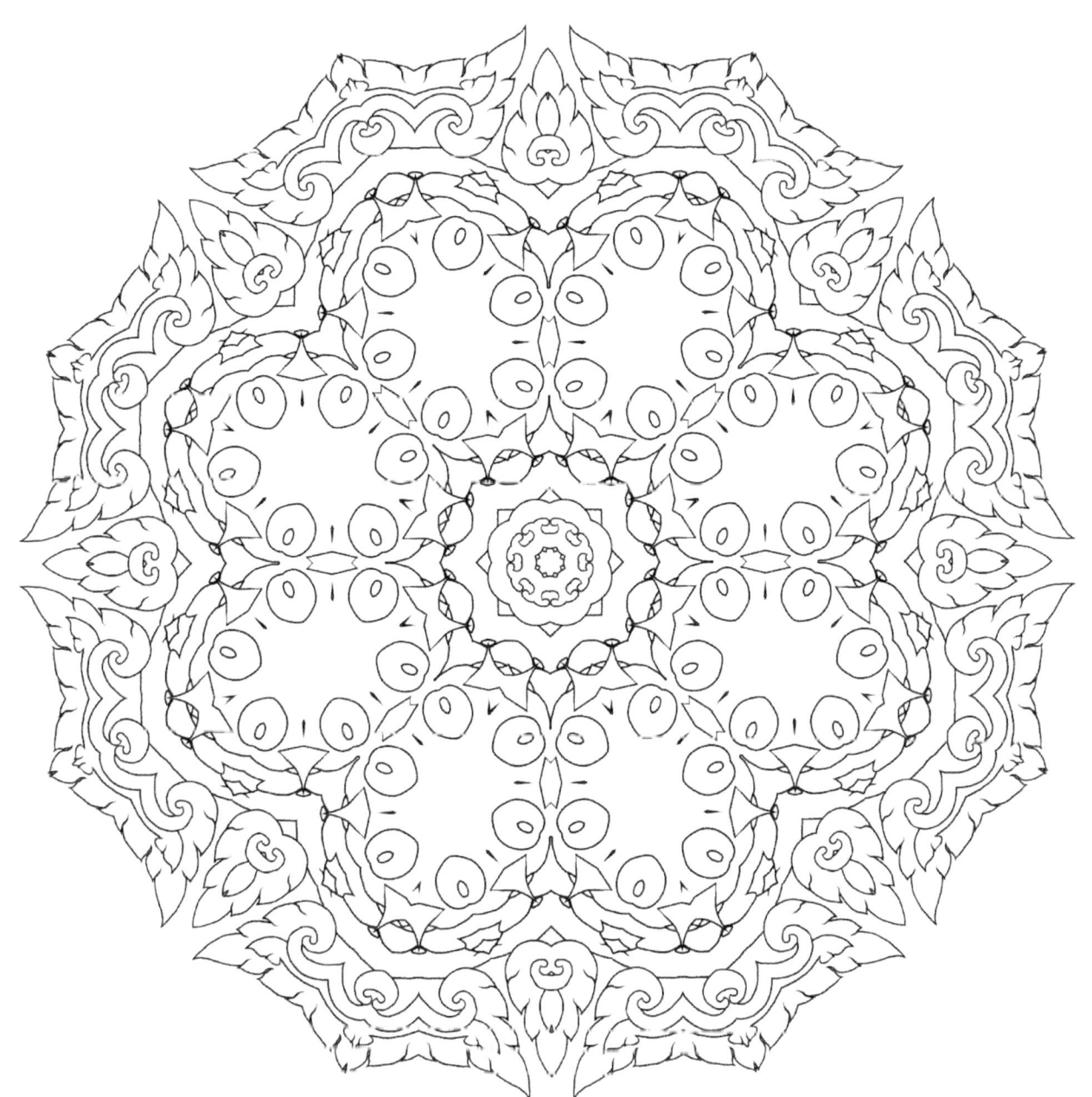

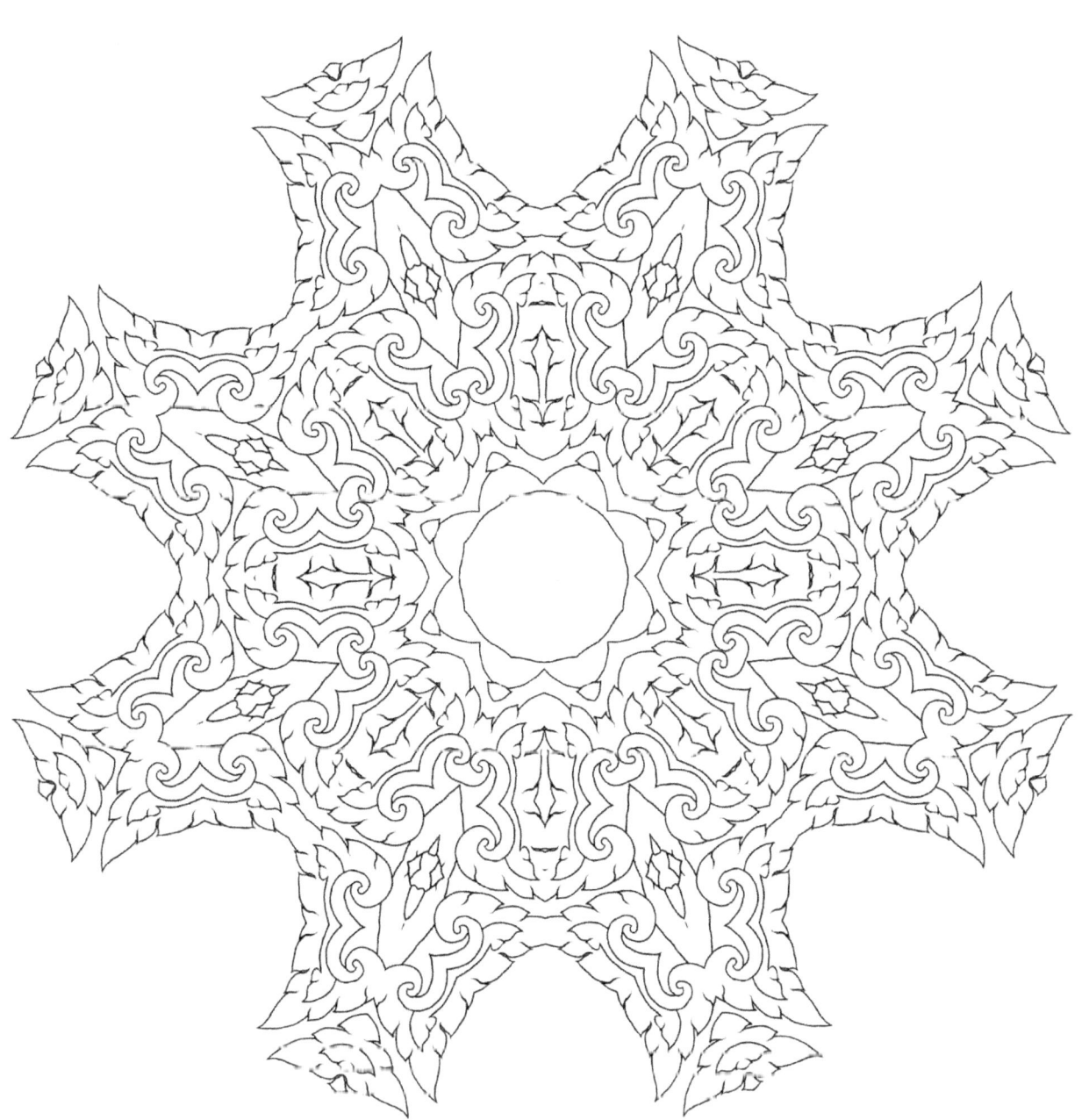

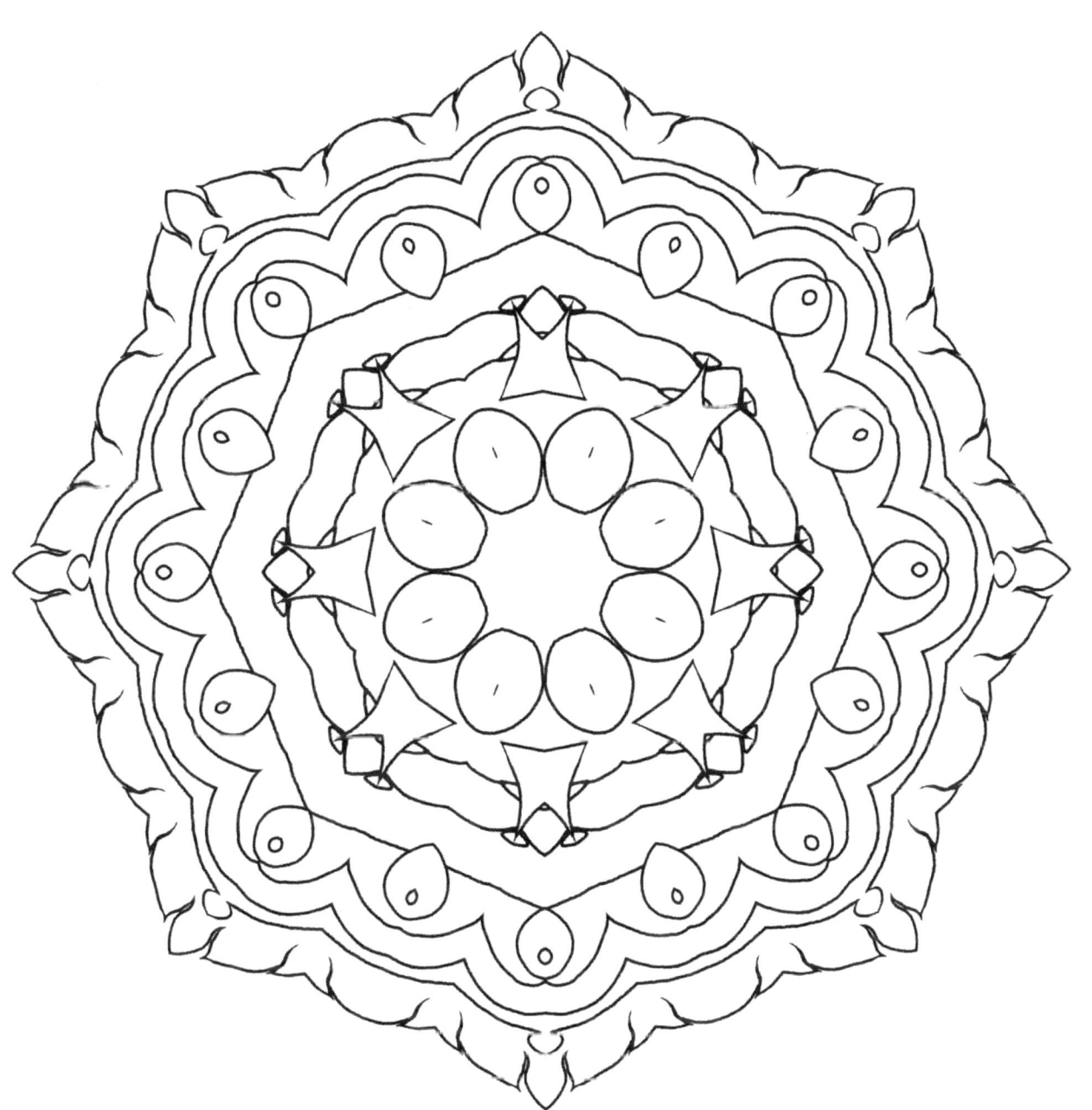

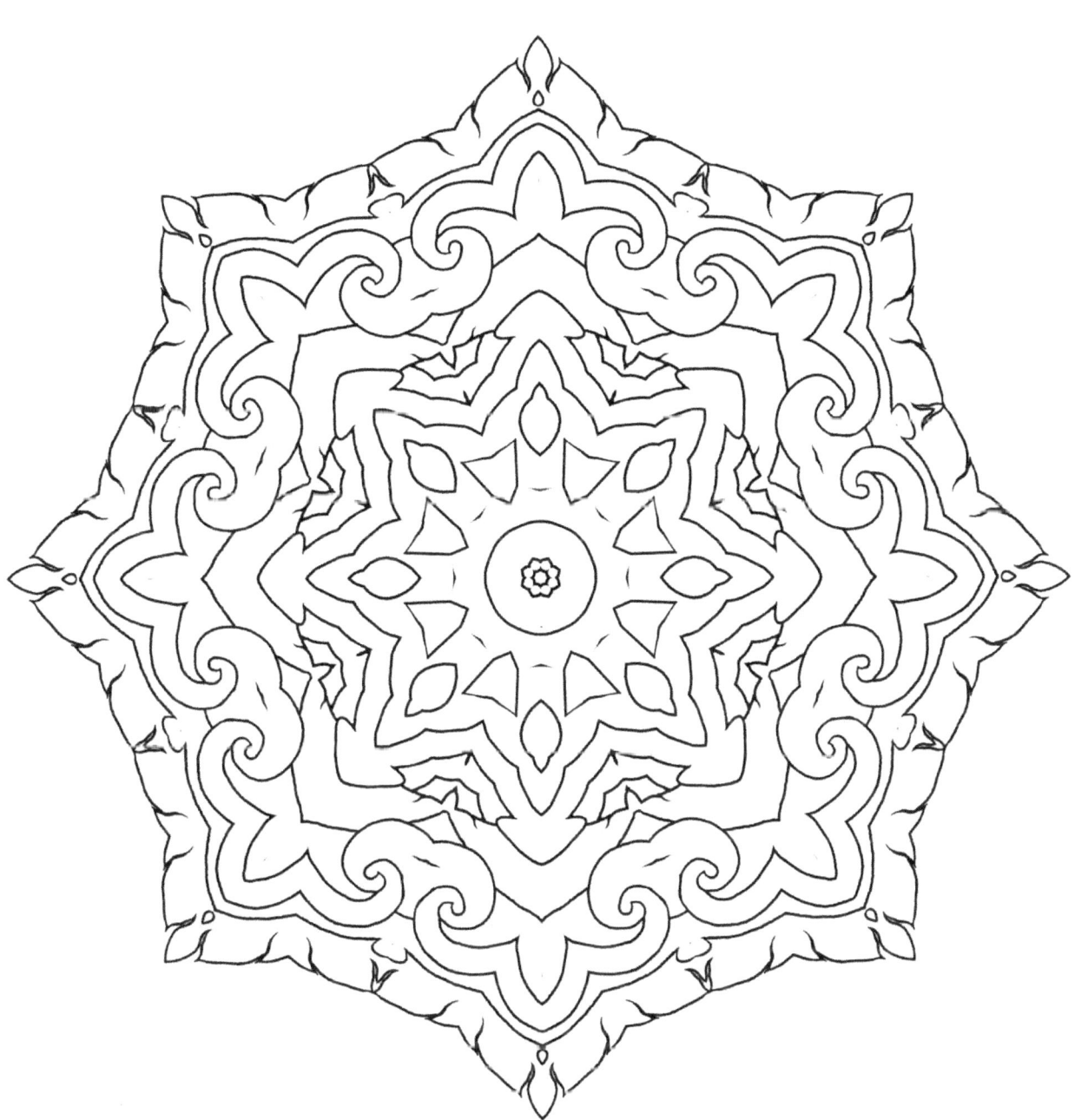

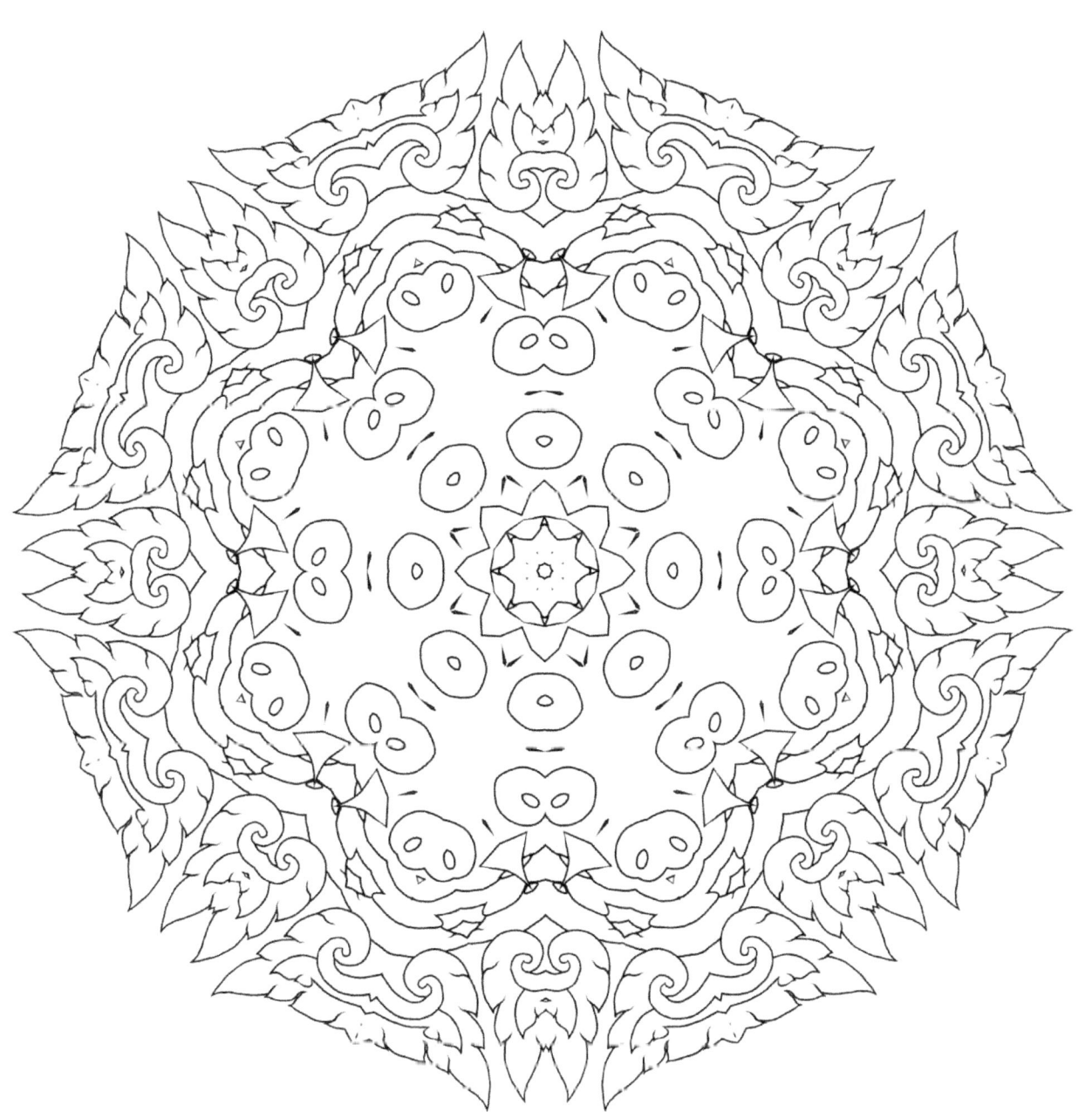

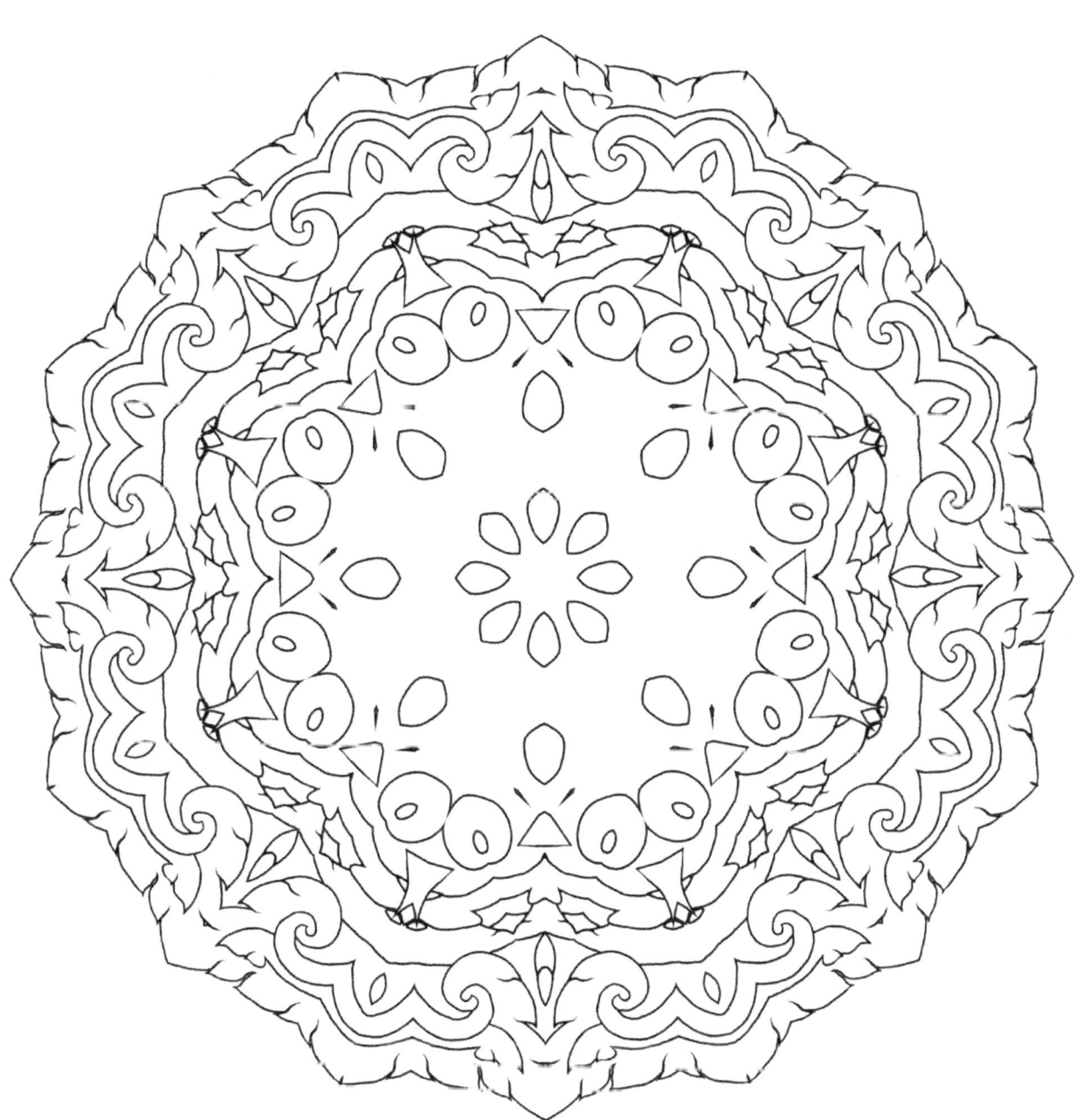

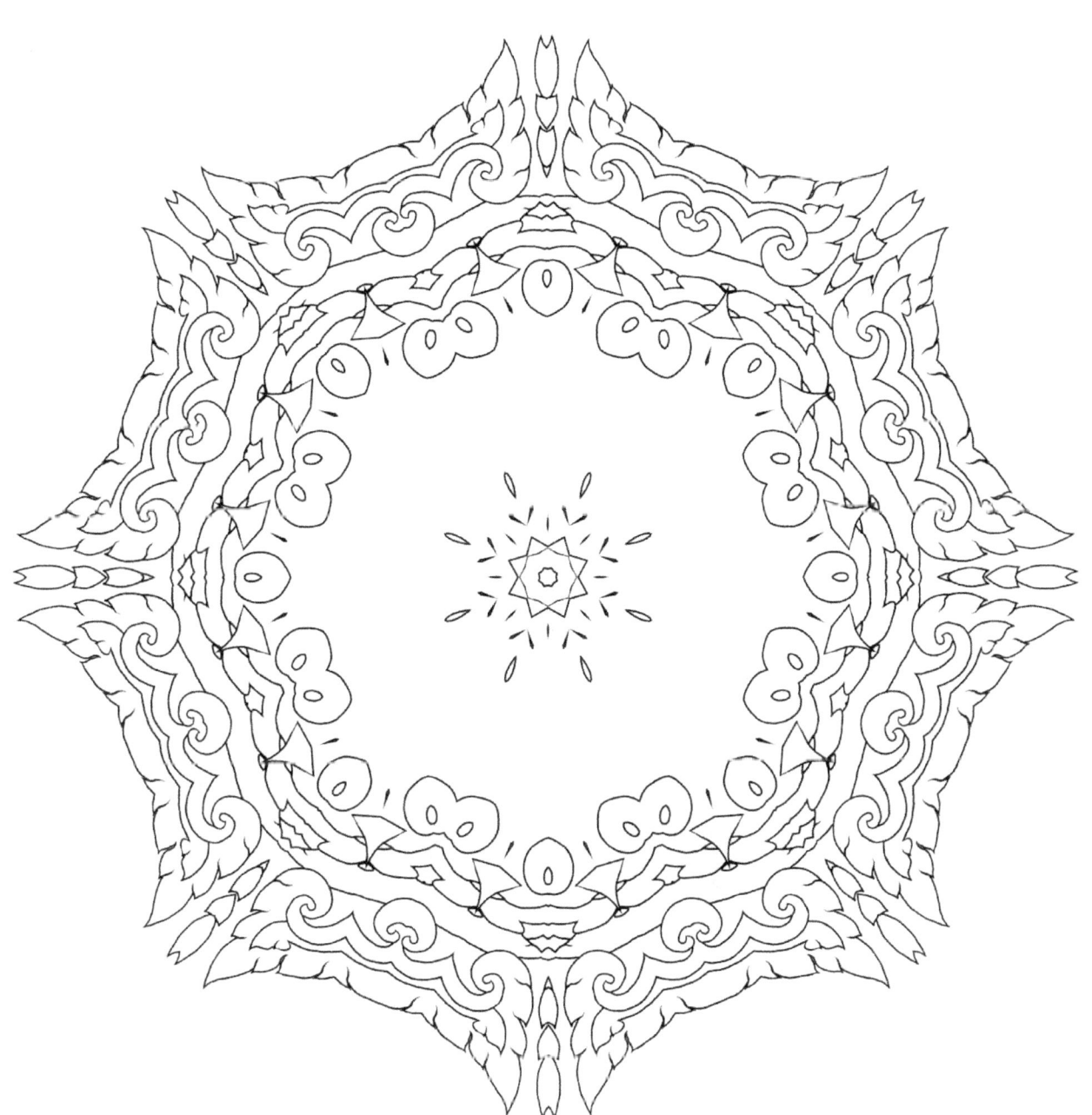

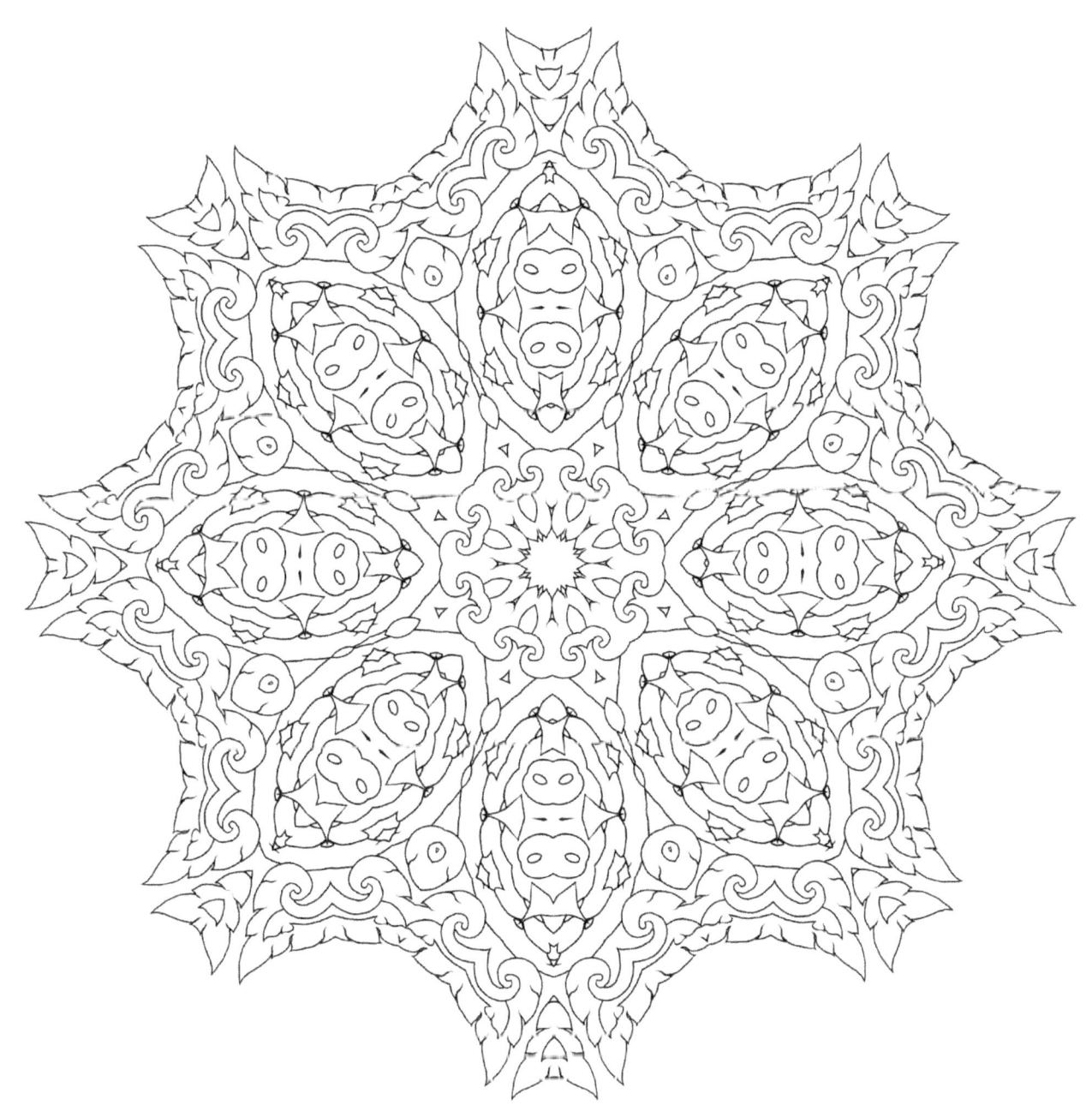

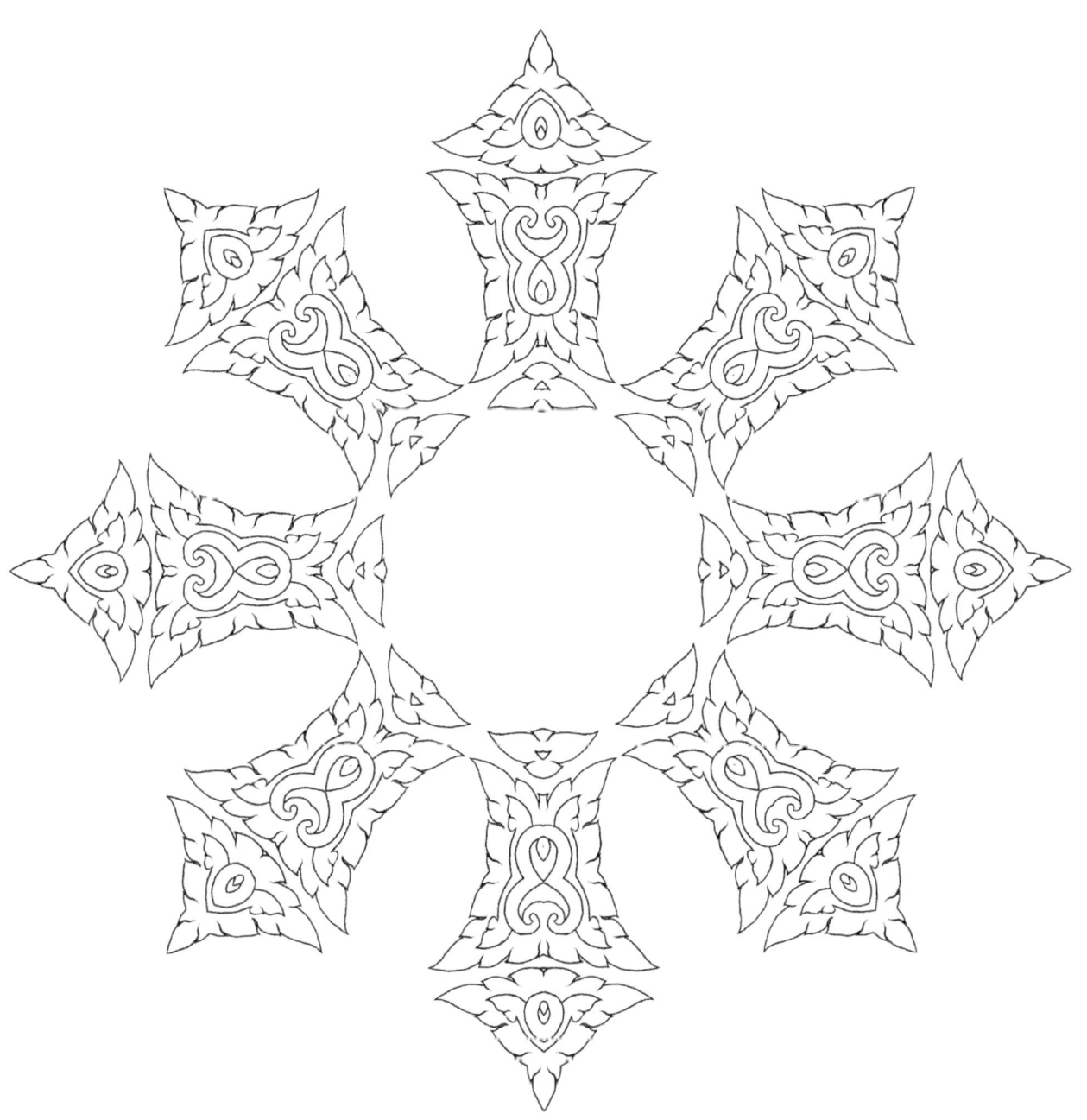

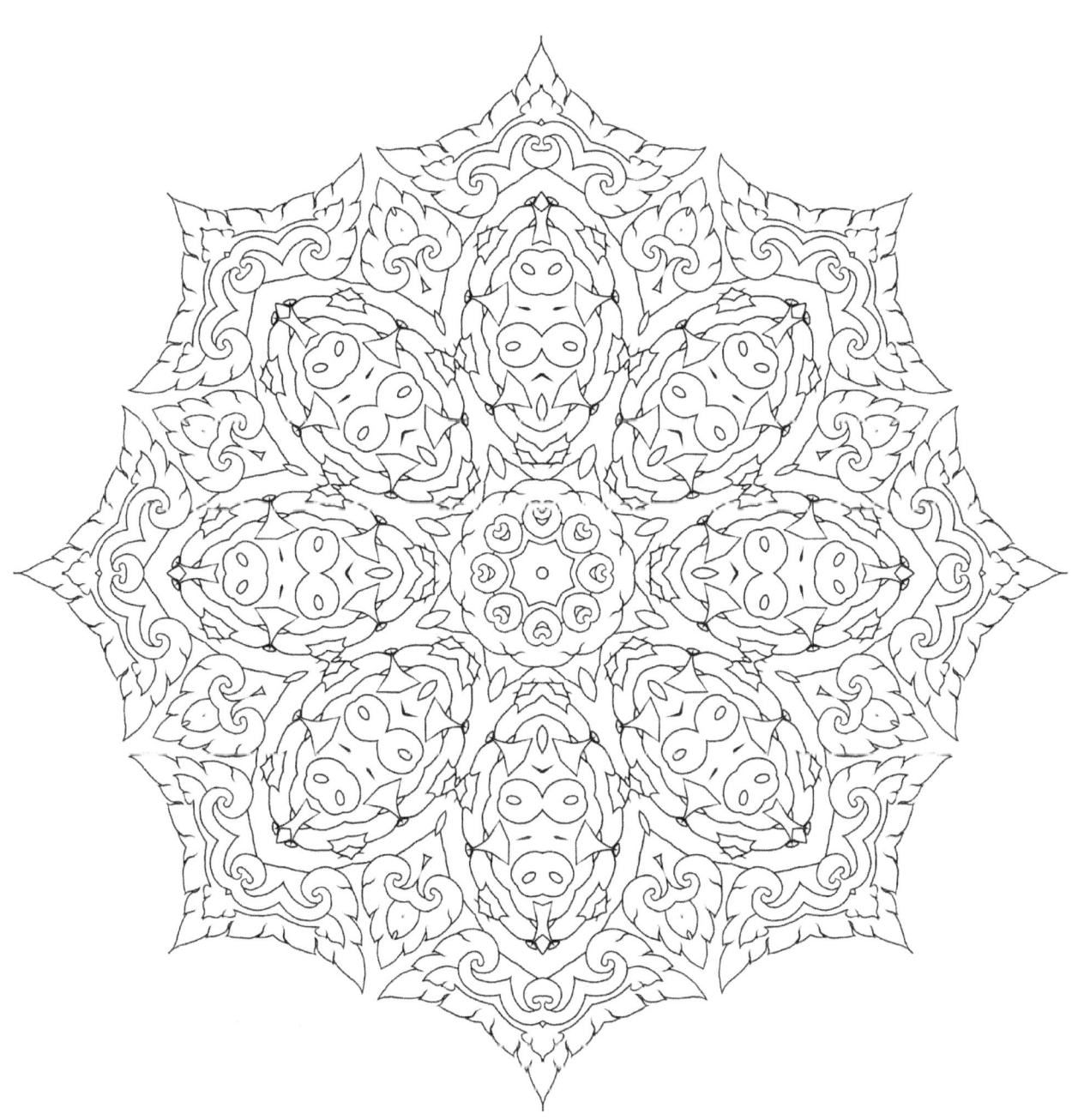

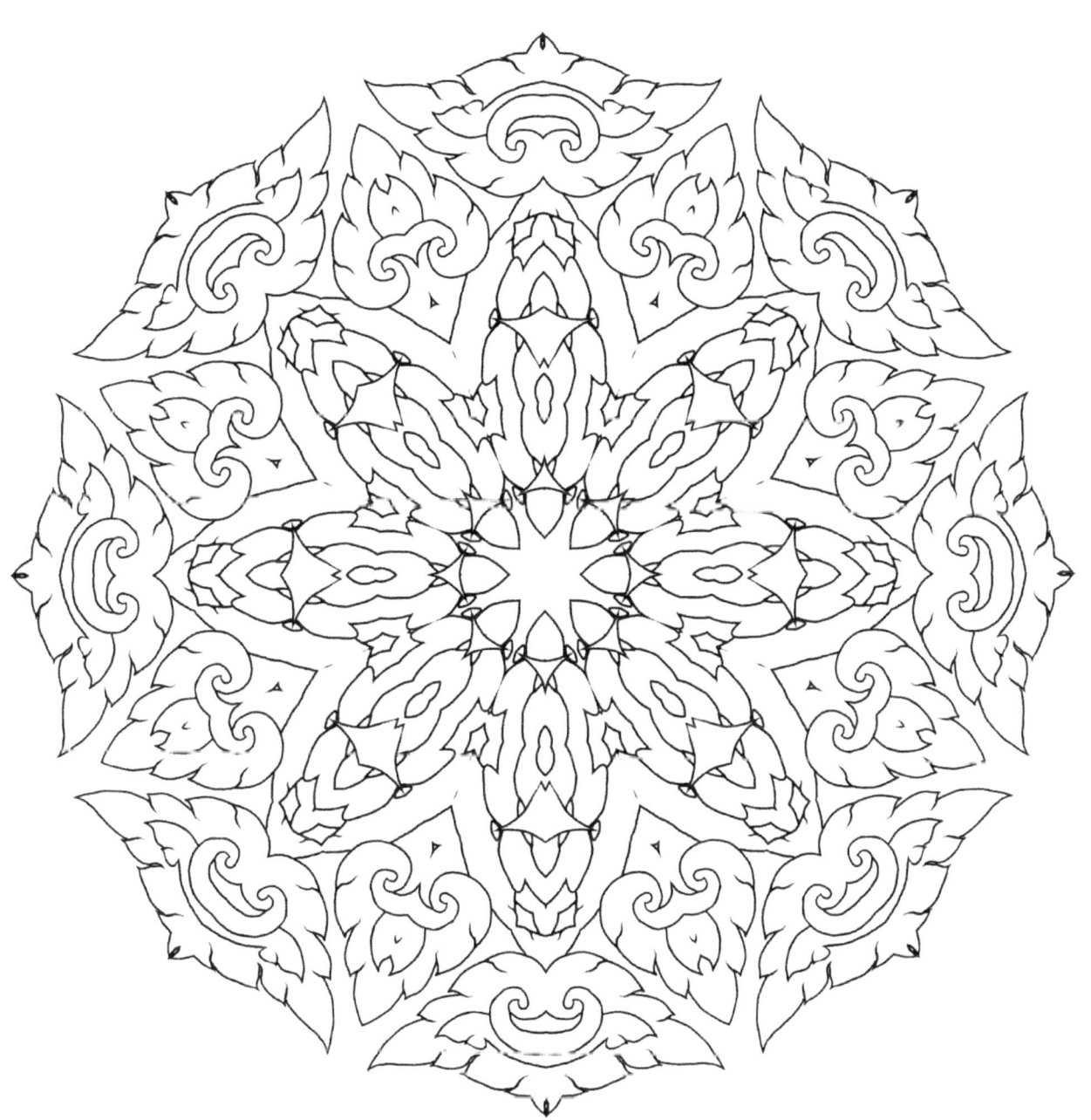

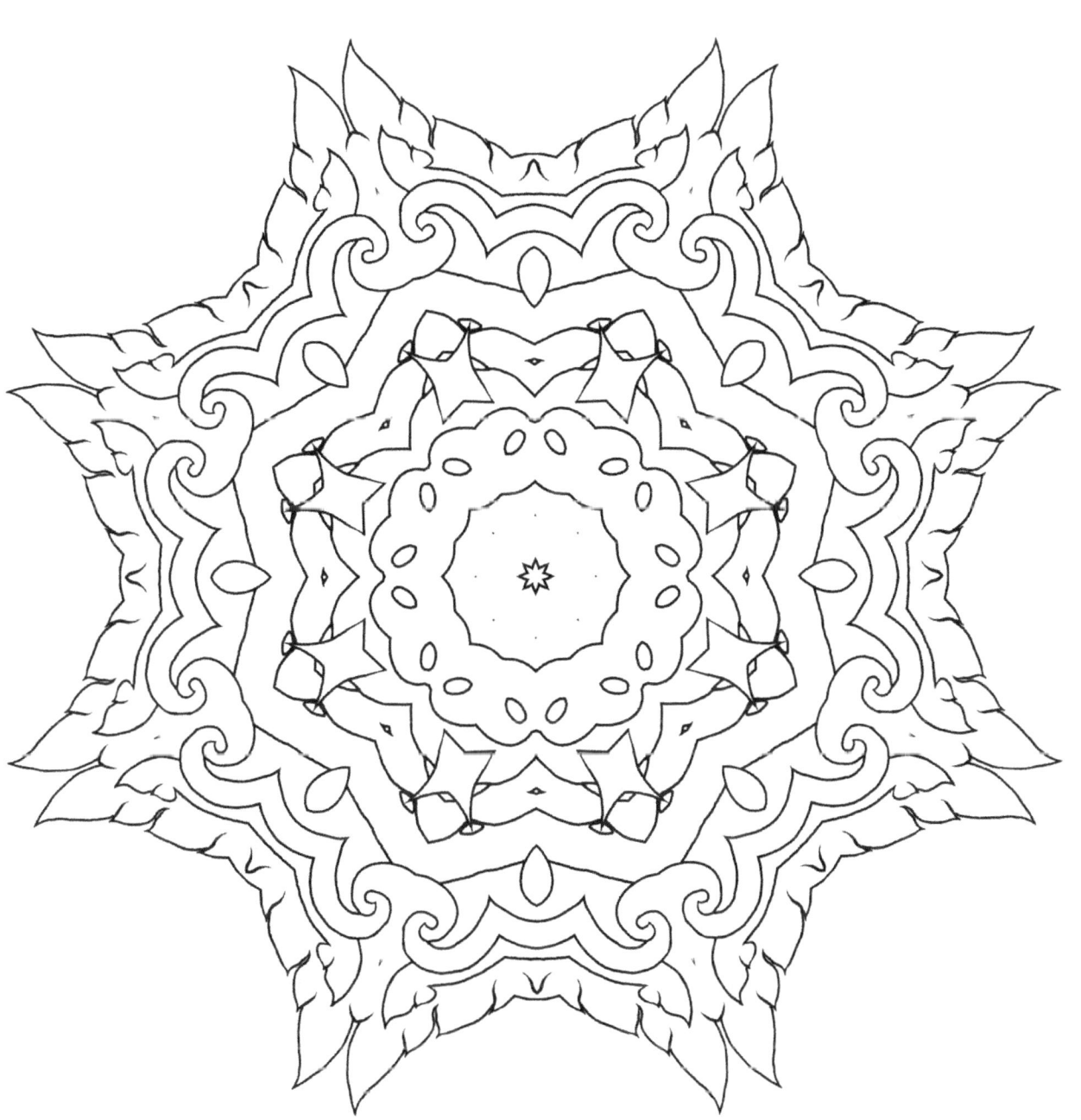

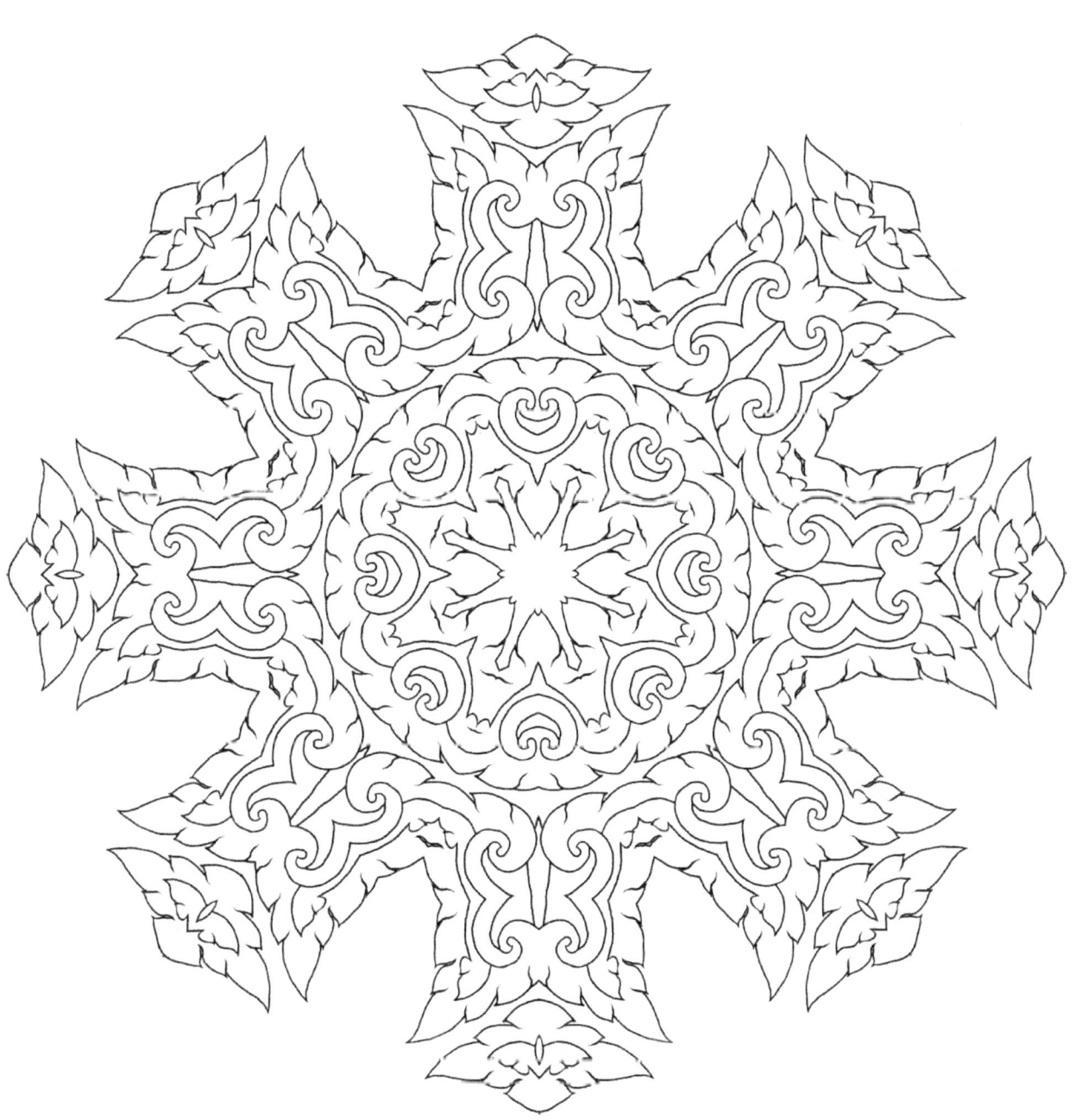

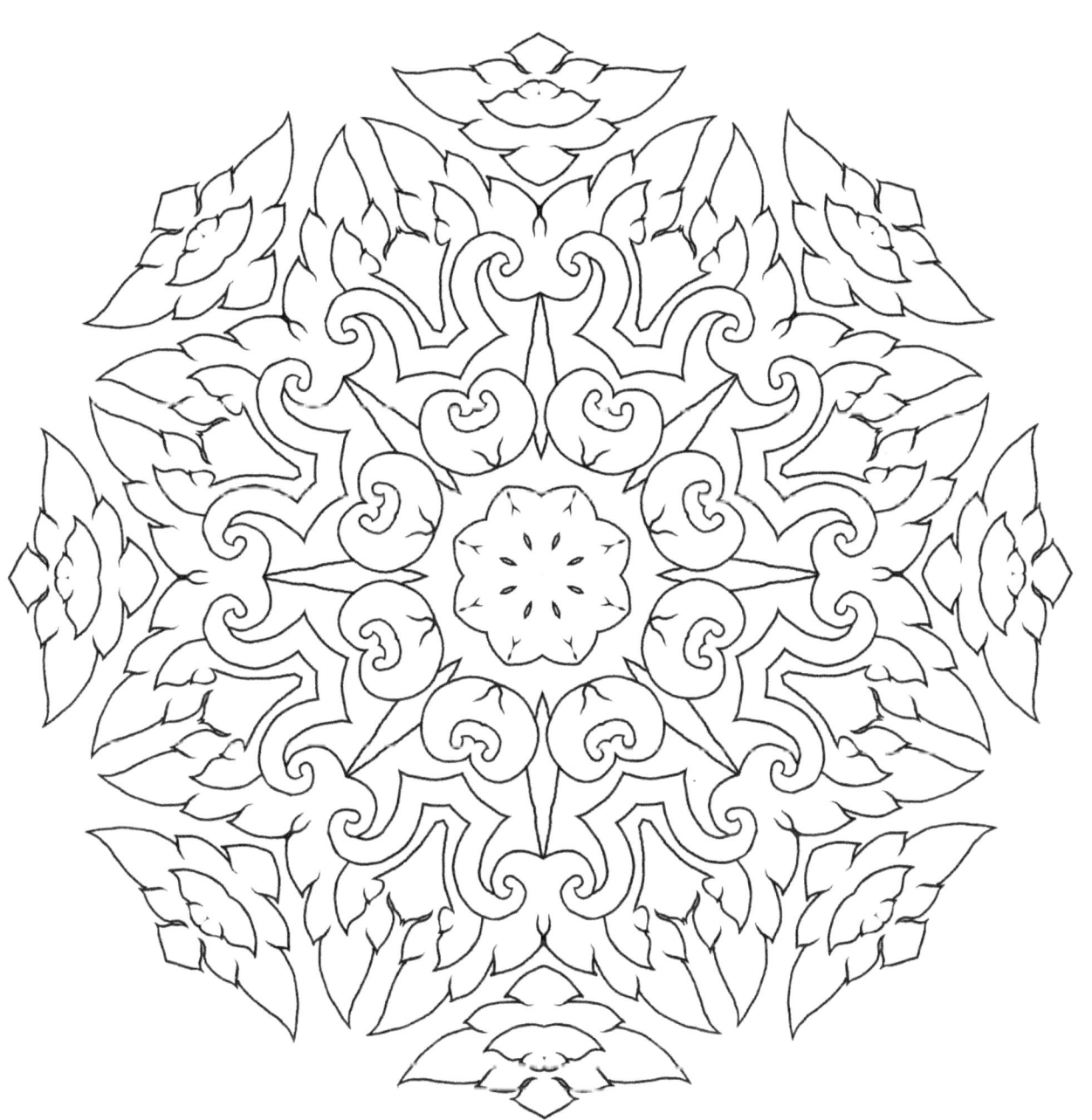

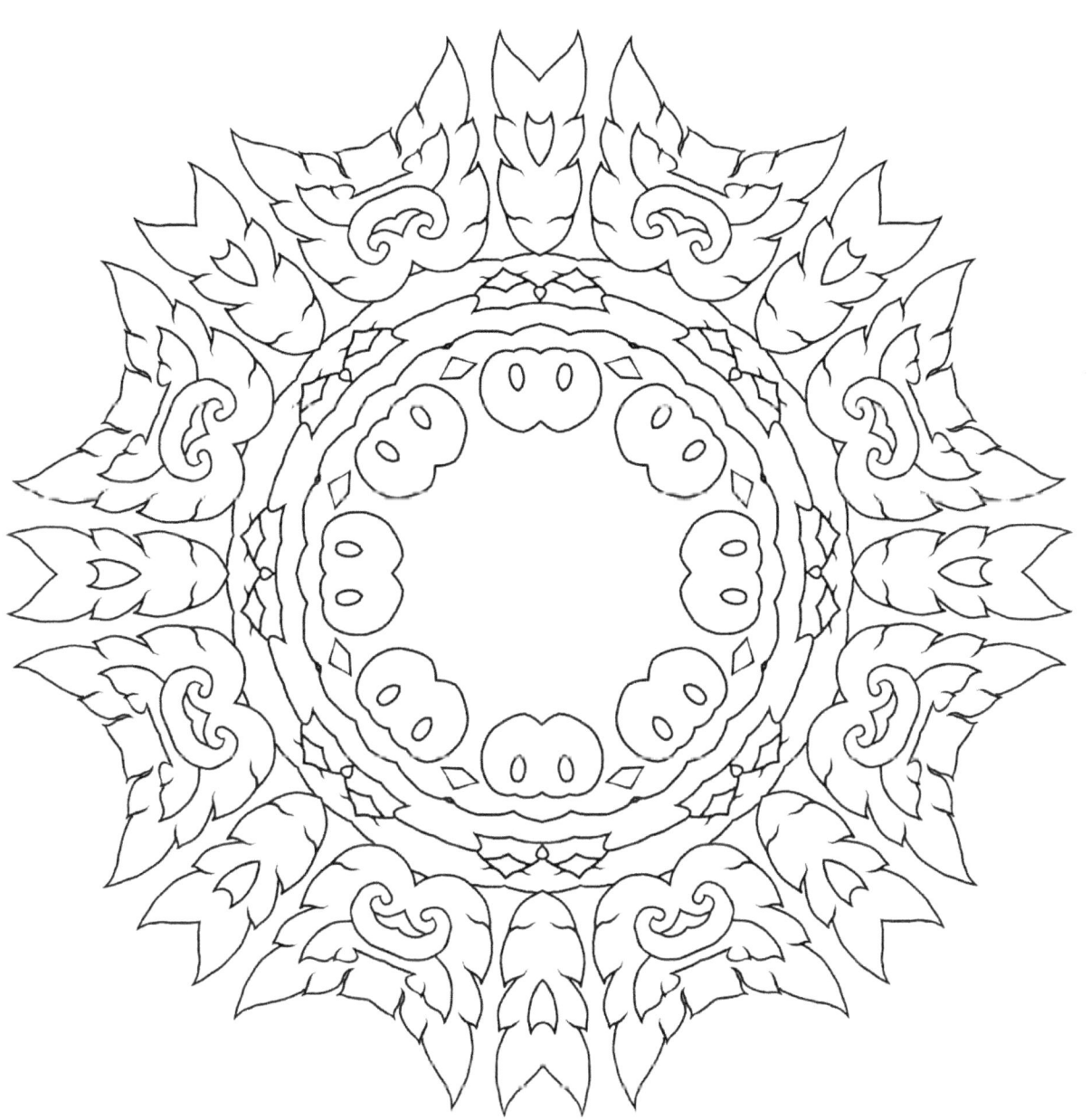

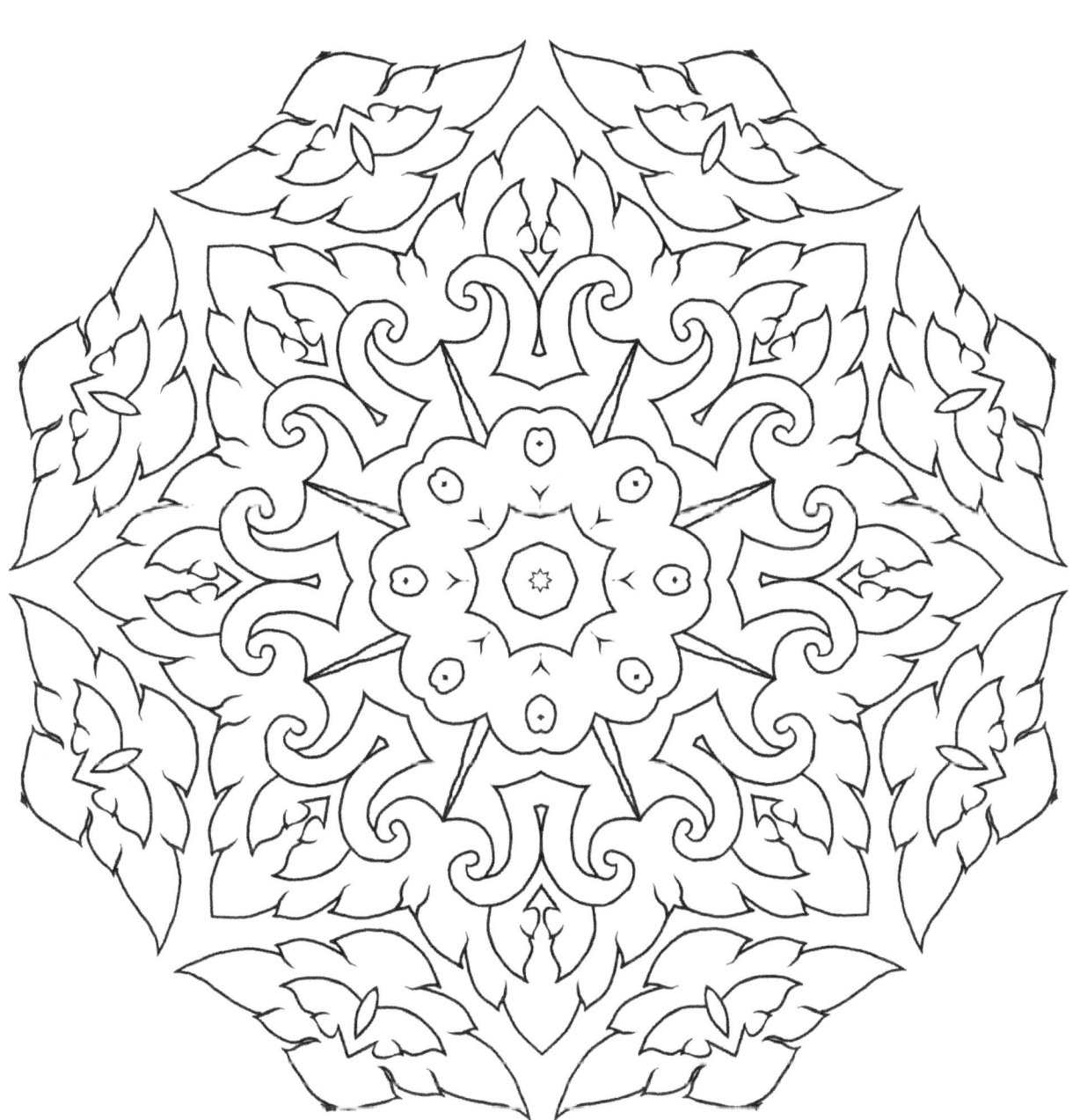

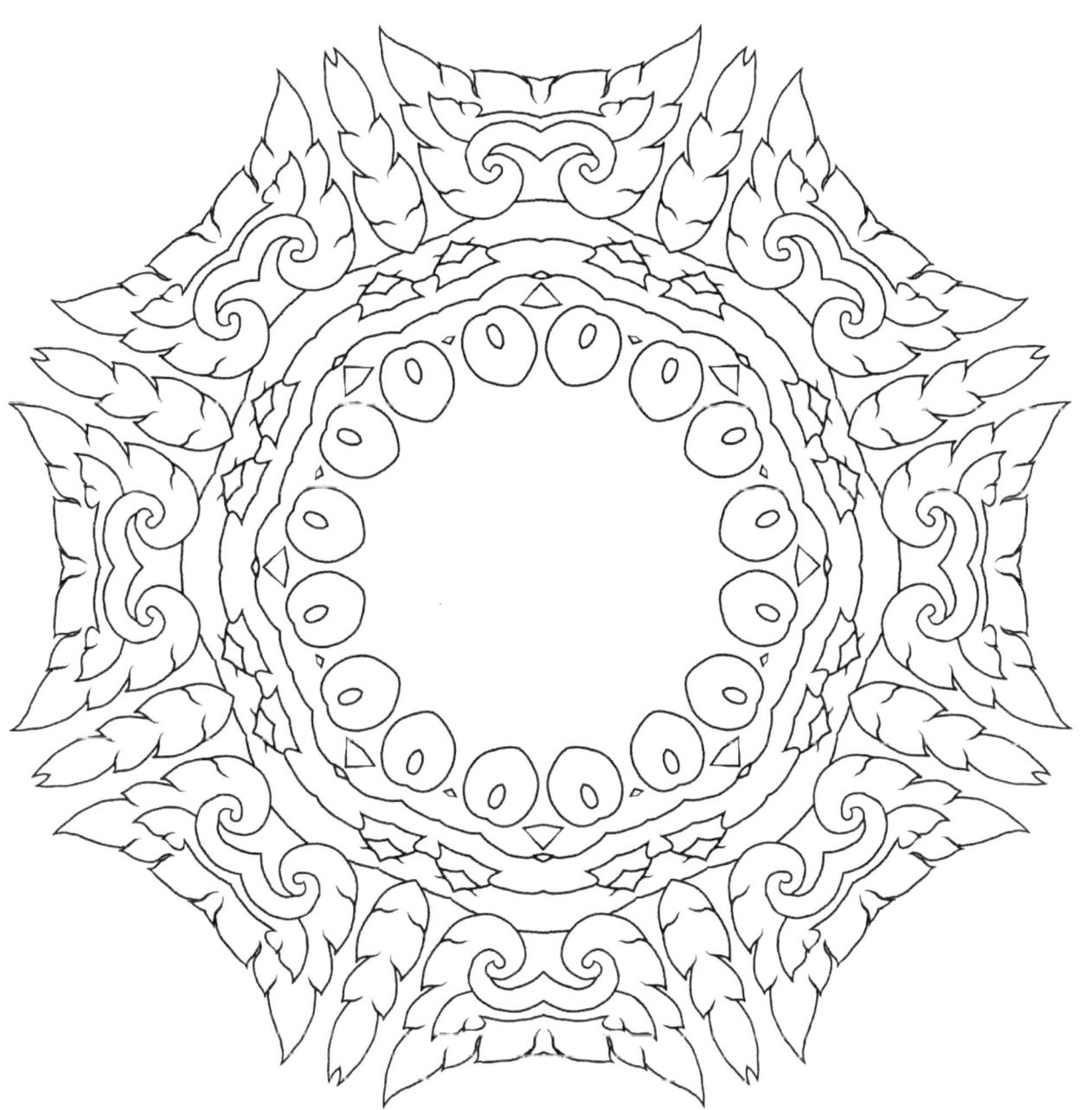

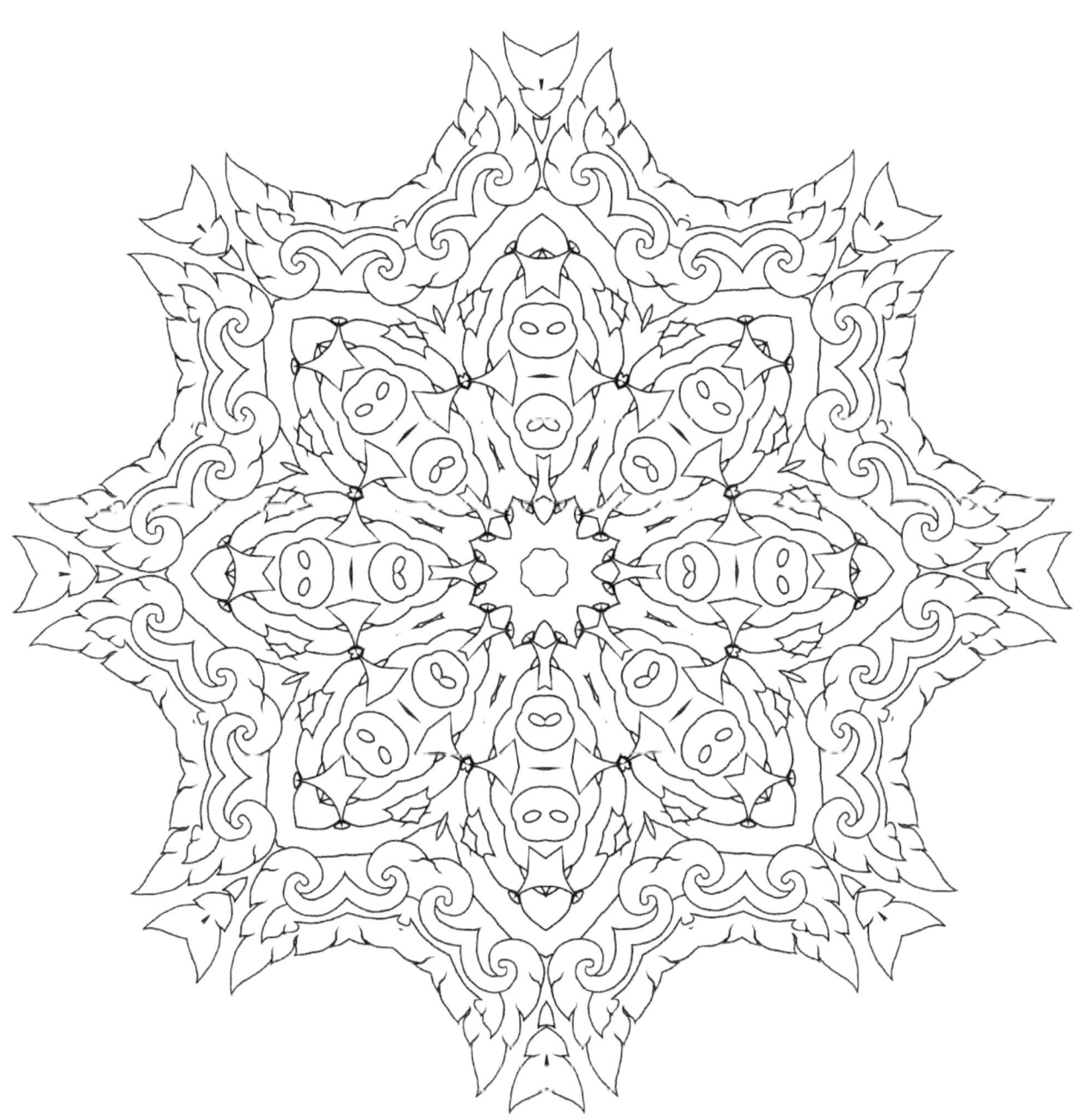

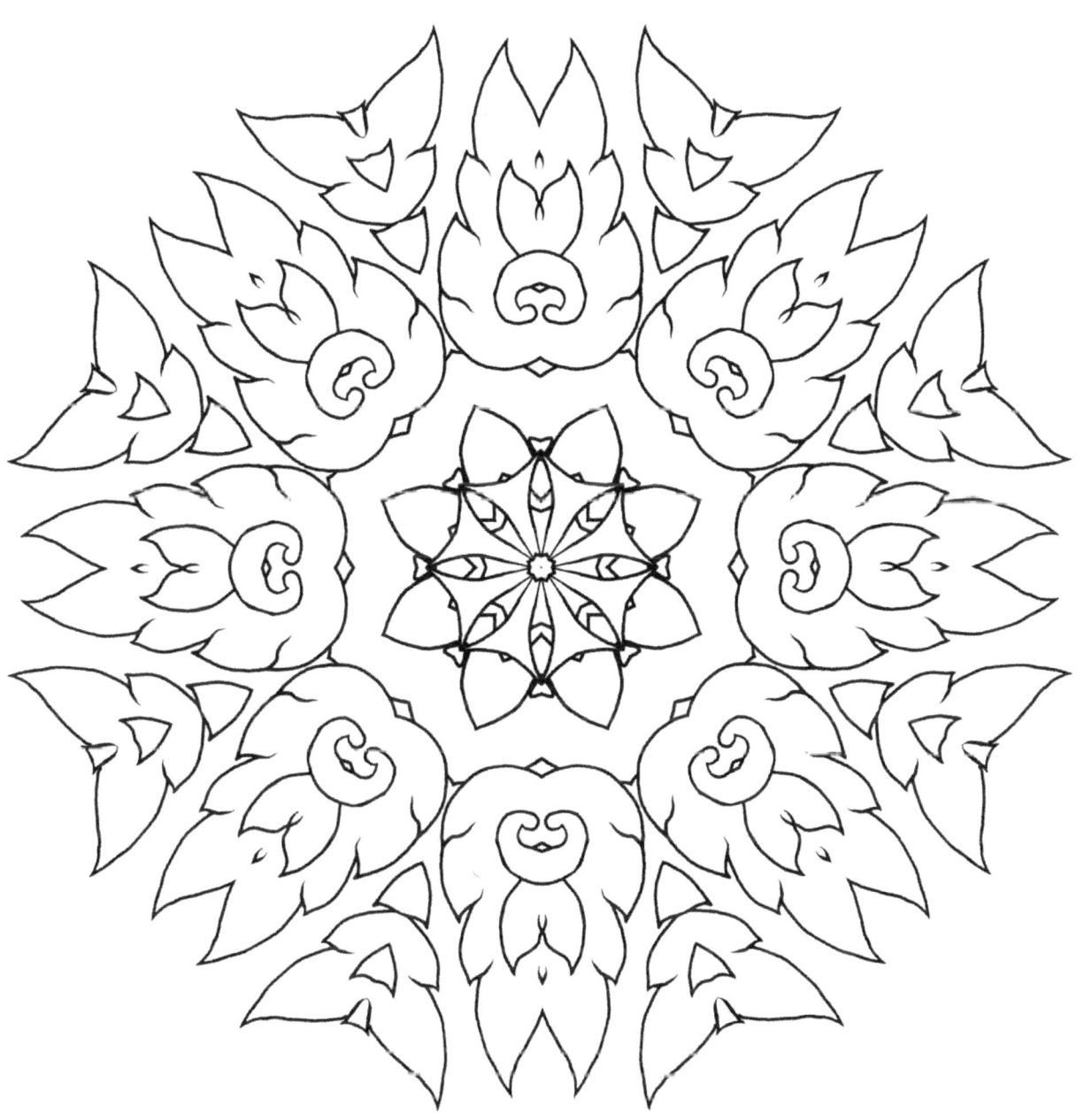

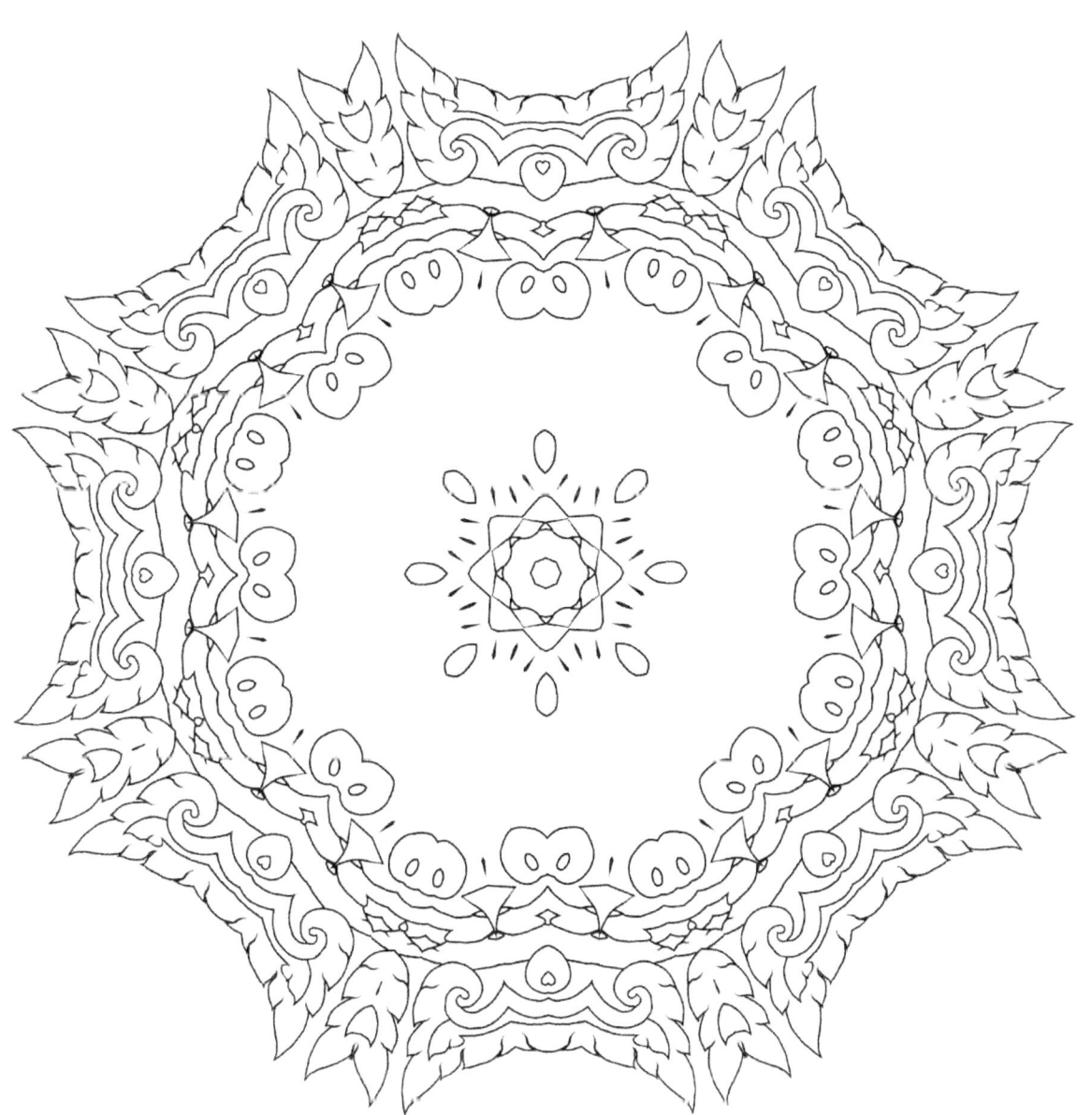

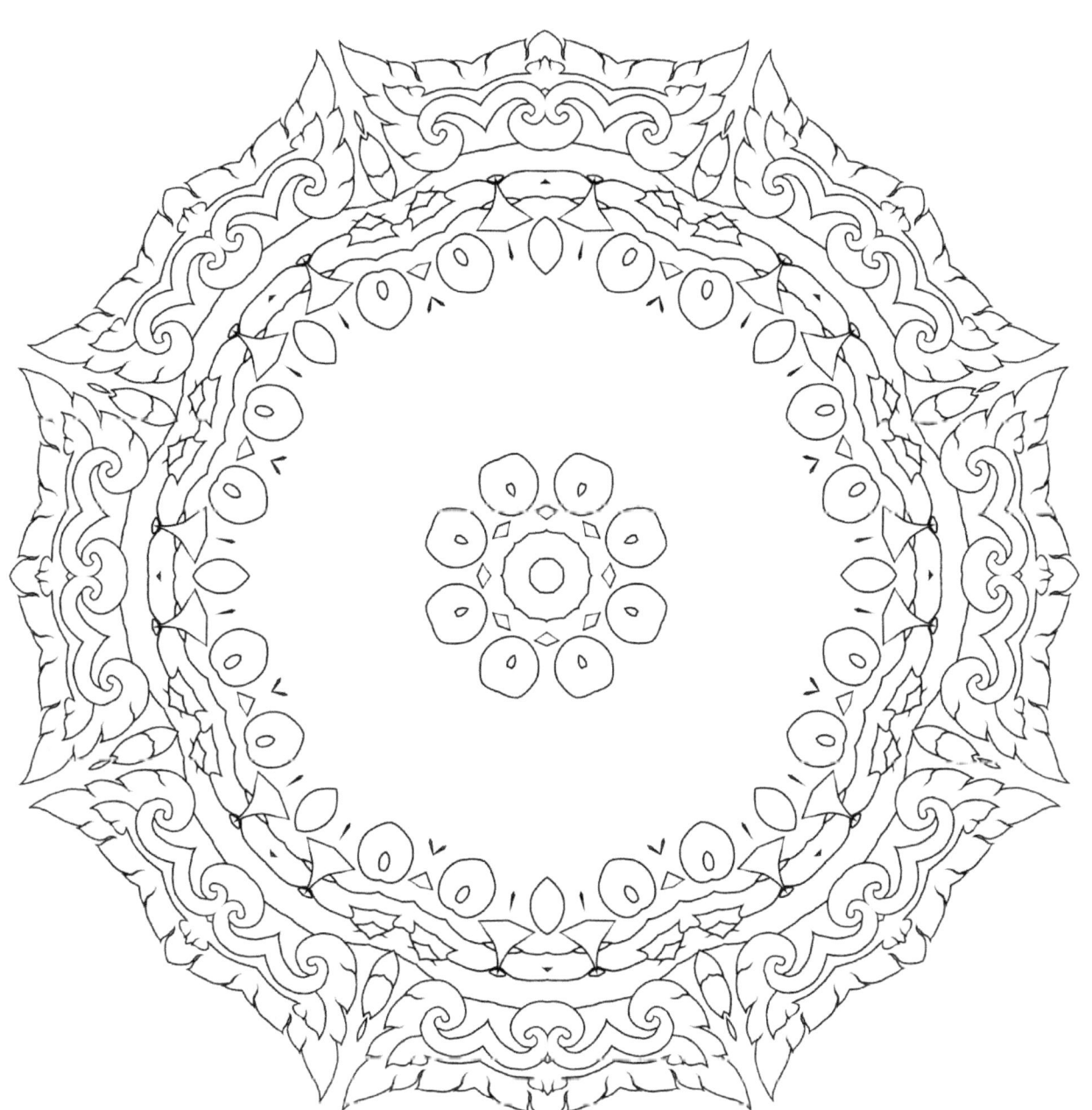

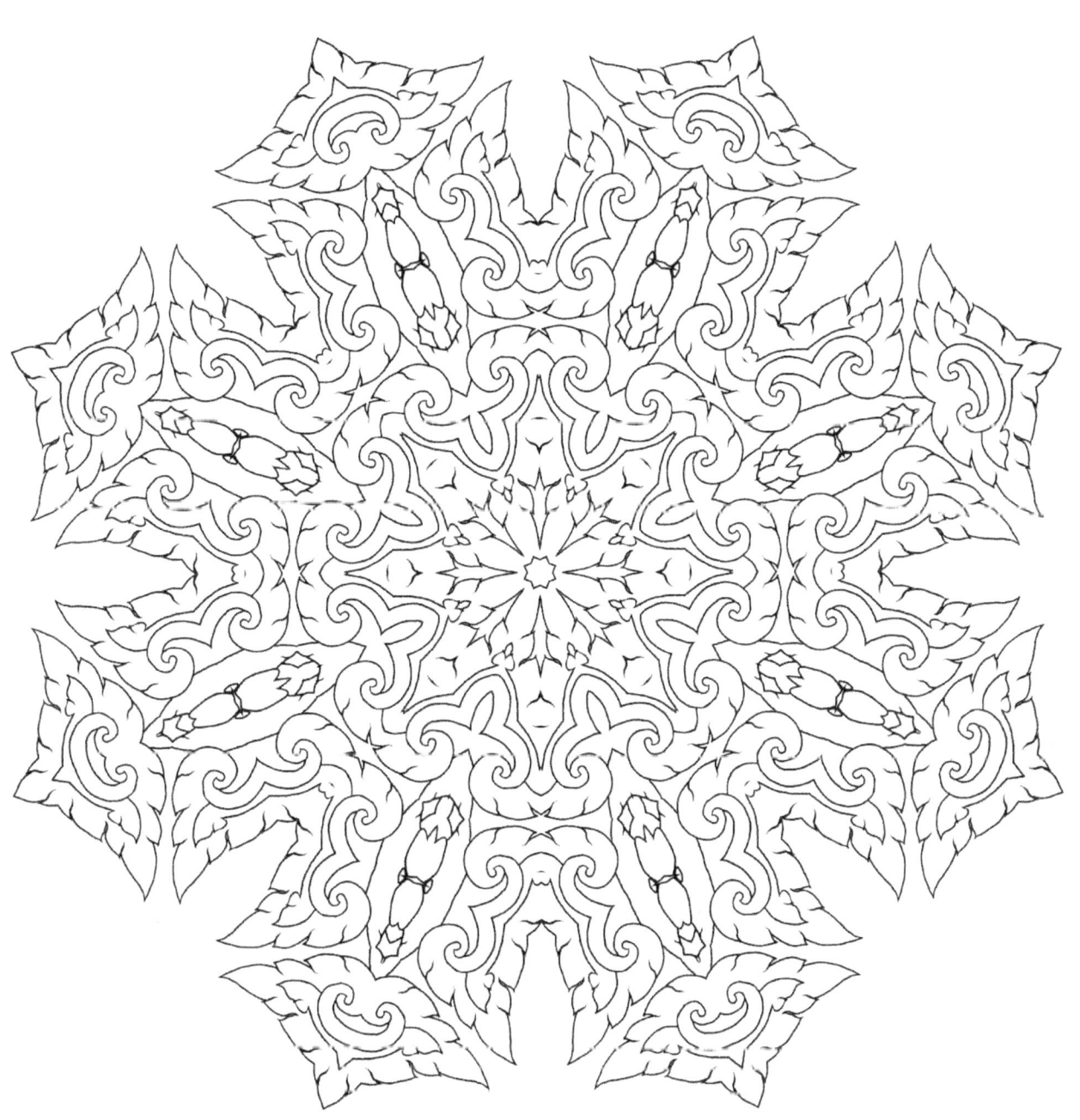

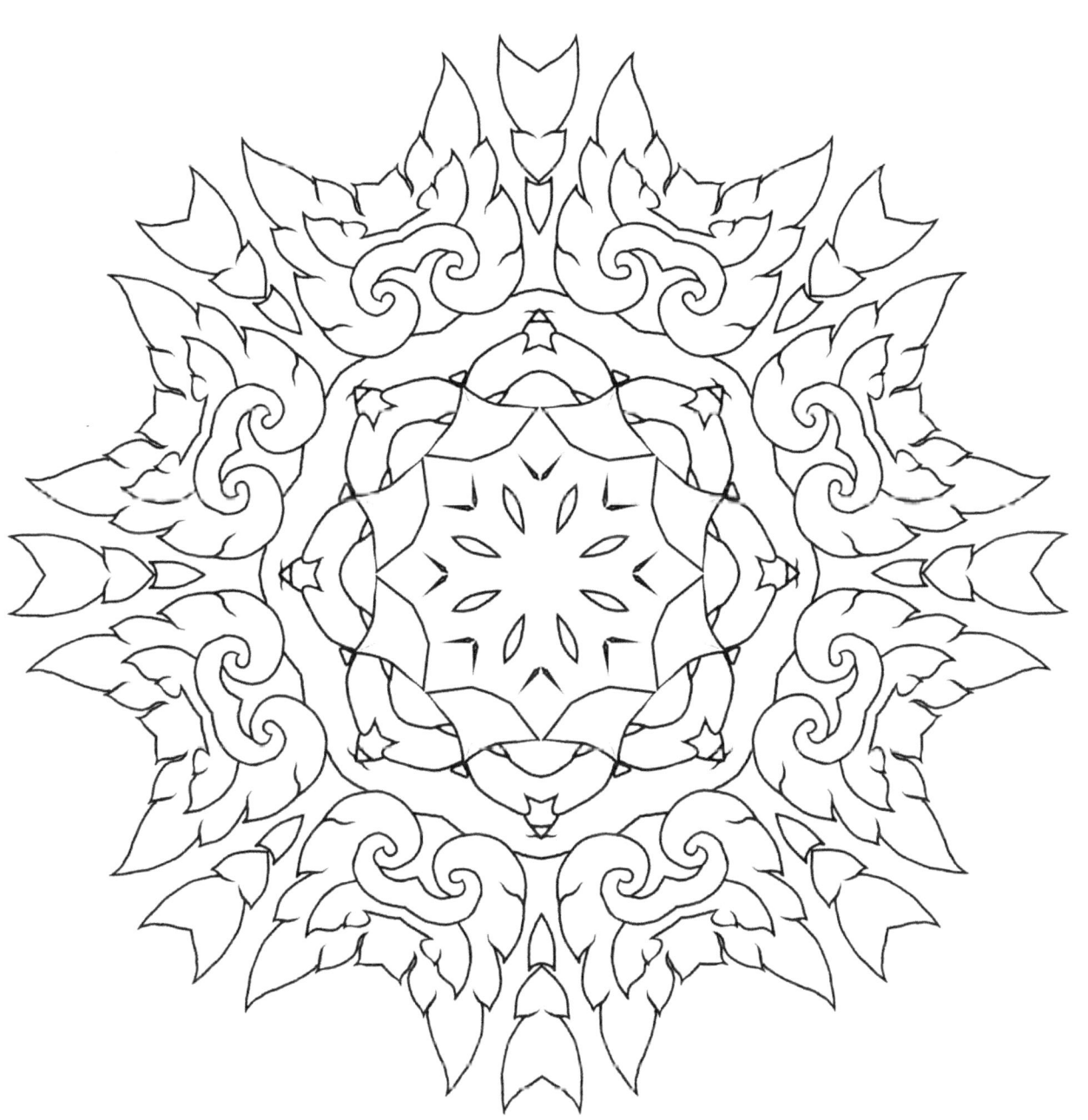

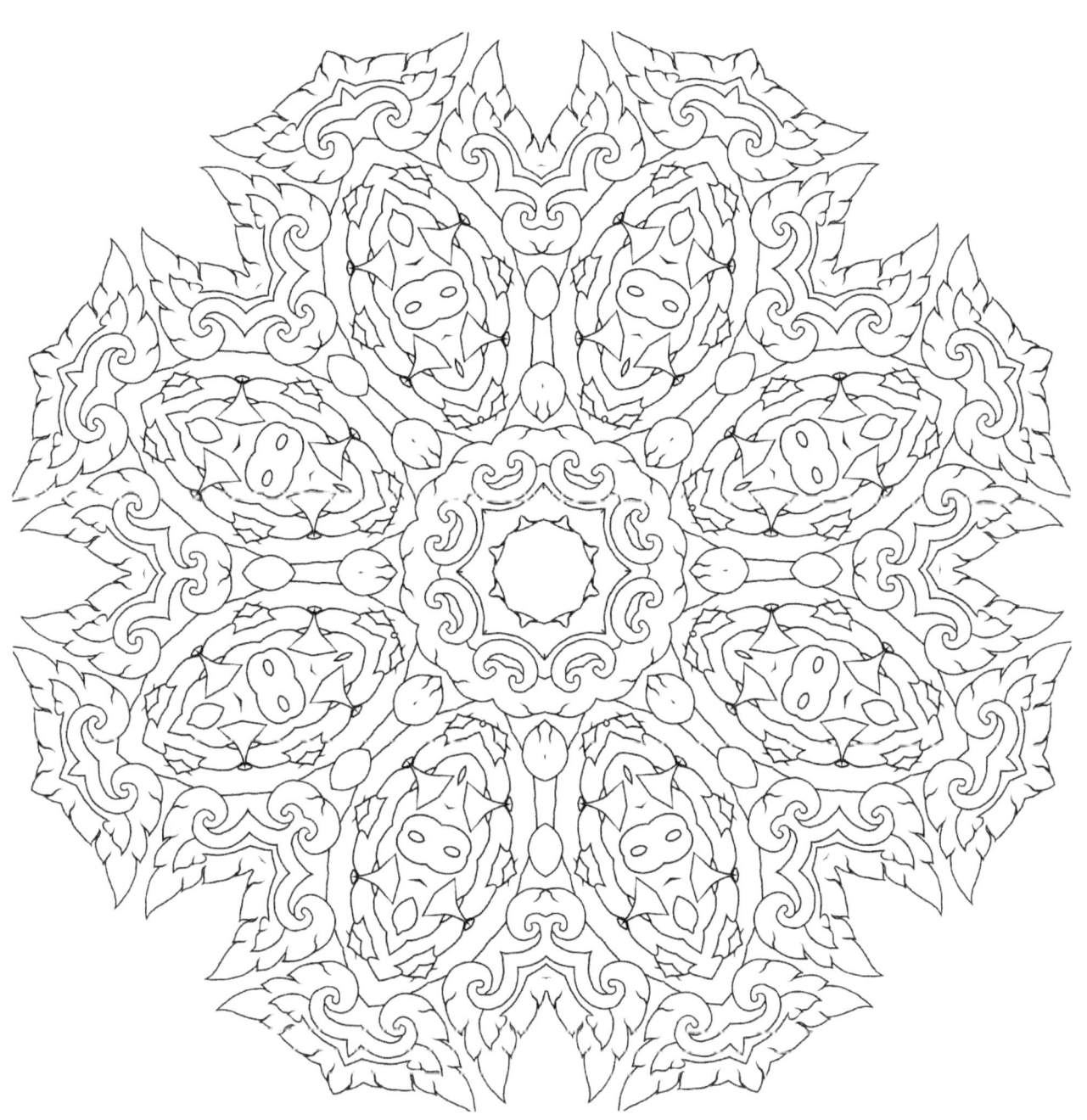

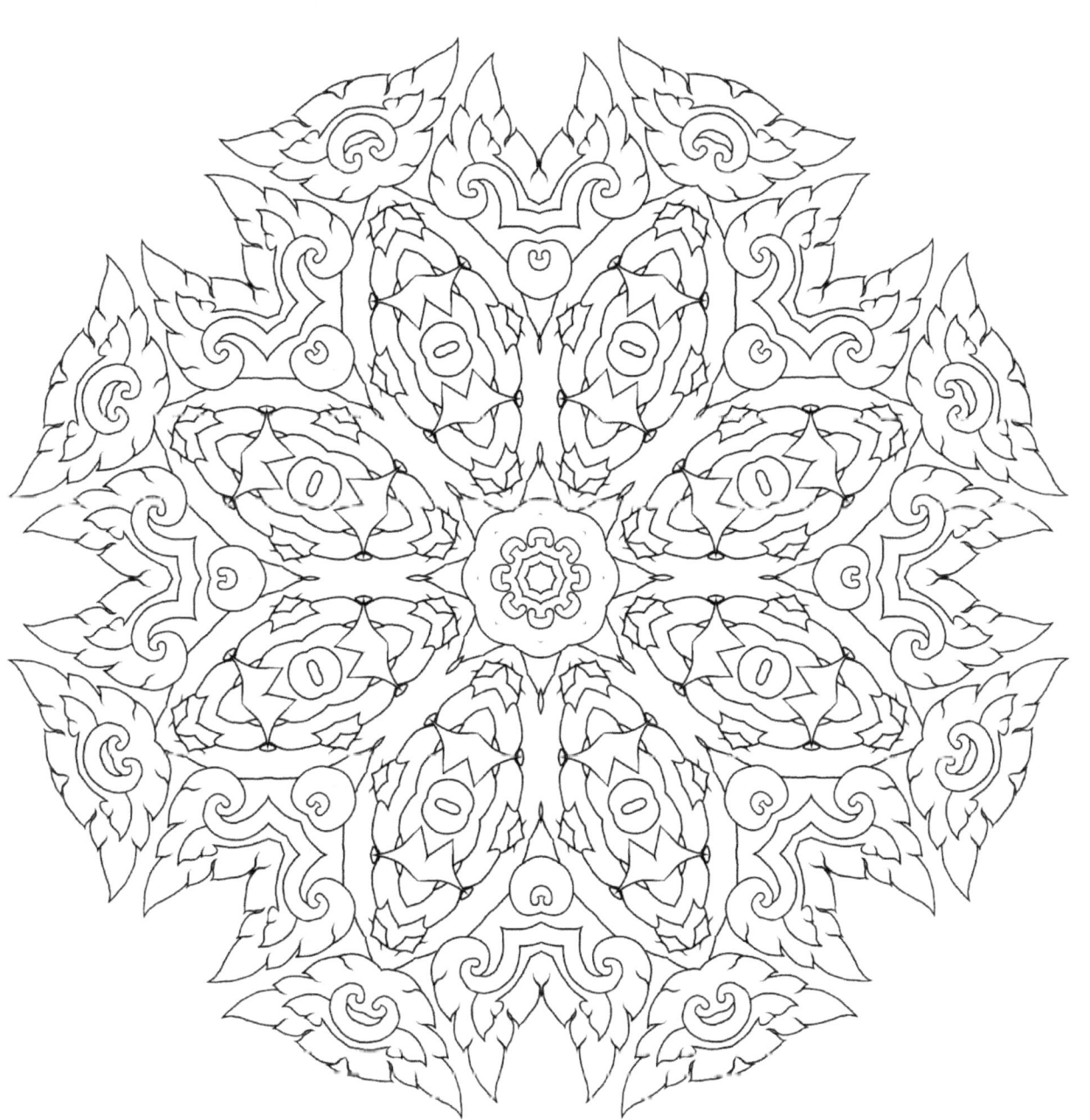

Thank you

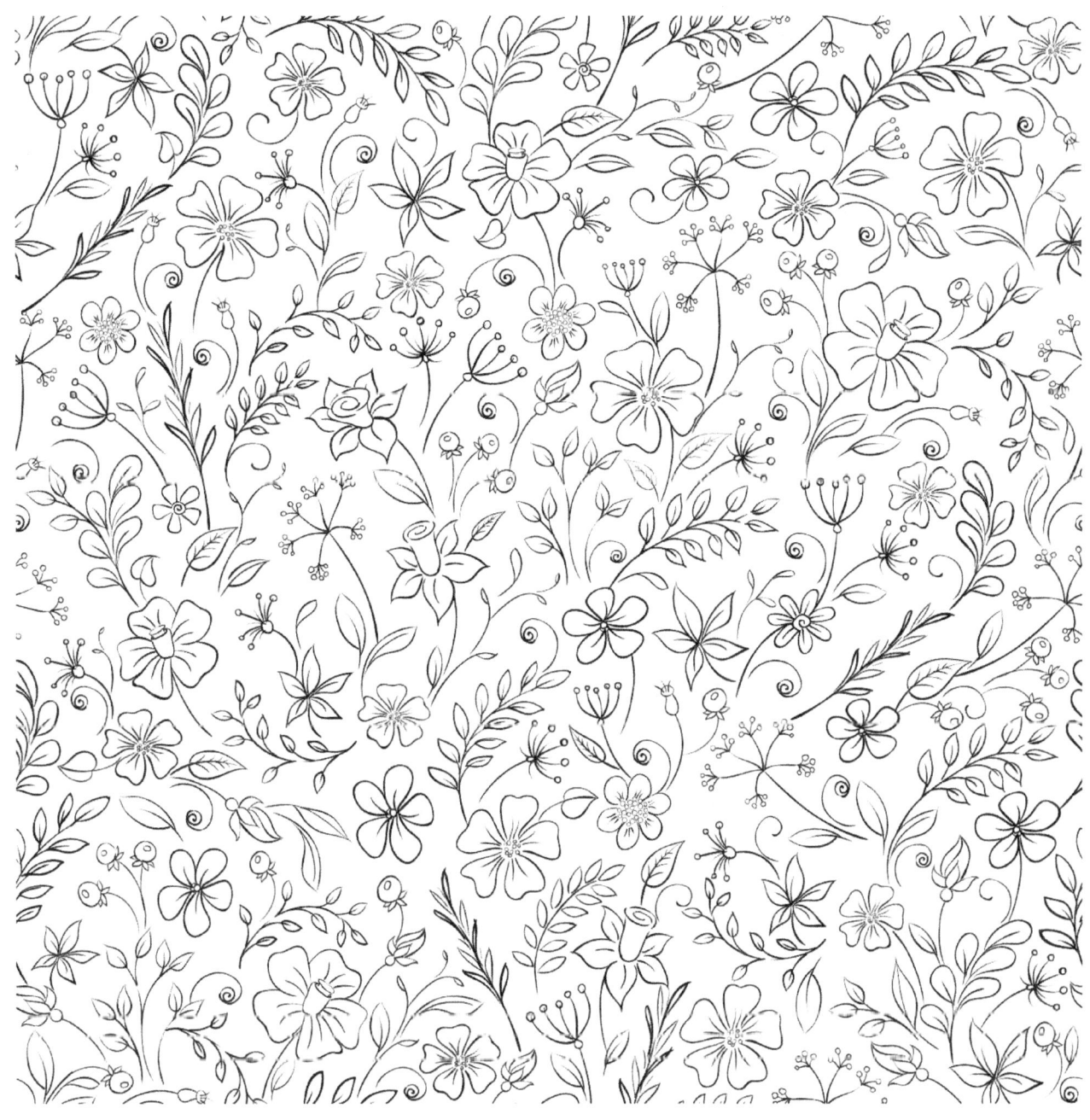

www.ingramcontent.com/pod-product-compliance
Lightning Source LLC
Chambersburg PA
CBHW081116180526
45170CB00008B/2864